EXTRAORDINARY ACHIEVEMENTS

Standing Tall

David S. Philemon

Royal Diadem Publishing Inc.

Dedication

To the Almighty God, my foundation and ever-present help. I am grateful for Your boundless love and grace that sustain me daily. And to my mentor in ministry, Rev. George Izunwa, whose steadfast commitment to the call of God has deeply impacted my life. Your guidance and support have been invaluable, encouraging me to walk boldly in the path God has set before me. Thank you for your example and your heart for the Kingdom.

Apostle Dr. David Philemon

ACKNOWLEDGMENT

This book would not have been possible without the unwavering support, dedication, and talent of an extraordinary team. My deepest gratitude goes to each of you for your contributions, insights, and encouragement throughout this journey.

First and foremost, thank you to Rev. Mimi Philemon my dear wife, Rev. Shina Gentry, and and my assistant pastor Rev. Bright Amudoaghan for your incredible effort, encouragement, and belief in this project. Your support has been instrumental in bringing this vision to life.

To the dedicated leaders of Royal Diadem Publishing, Ide Imogie and Kishawna Bailey, I am immensely grateful for your belief in this project from the very beginning and for investing your time and energy into its development. Your creativity, dedication, and expertise have been the backbone of this endeavor.

I am especially grateful to the Royal Diadem Publishing team— Beulah Orogun, Emmanuella Ben-Eboh, Doyinsade Awodele, Kim Matthews, and Shante Gill, for your meticulous attention to detail, refining every page and ensuring that each word reflects our vision.

A heartfelt thank you to my family, friends, and colleagues whose unwavering support and belief in this project gave me the courage and strength to see it through.

Finally, thank you to all the readers and supporters who make this work meaningful. I am humbled and honored to share this journey with each of you.

With all my gratitude,
David Philemon

Apostle Dr. David Philemon

CONTENTS

INTRODUCTION

Embracing A Radical Mindset

I n our journey of faith, we are called to stand tall. This means being strong and confident in our beliefs, even when faced with challenges. Standing tall is about our physical presence, inner strength, and commitment to God.

We live in a world that can sometimes push us to fit in or follow what everyone else is doing. But God wants us to be radical, so we should be willing to go against the flow and stand for what is right. Being radical in our faith means understanding God's heart and deciding to follow Him, even if it means standing alone.

The Bible tells us in *Daniel 3:14* (NIV), *"Nebuchadnezzar spoke to them, saying, 'Is it true, Shadrach, Meshach, and Abednego, that you do not serve my gods or worship the golden statue I have set up?'"* about three young men, Shadrach, Meshach, and Abednego.

They refused to bow down to a golden statue because they knew it was wrong. Instead of resisting pressure, they chose to stand tall for their faith in God. This story teaches us that God honors those who stand for Him, even when complicated.

Prayer is one of the most essential tools in our faith journey. Prayer is our way of communicating with God. It sustains us and gives us strength. *1 Thessalonians 5:17* (NIV) instructs, *"pray without ceasing."*

This means we should always be in a prayerful mindset, seeking God's guidance and strength in every situation. If we have the Word of God but do not pray, we are like a teacher who has knowledge but does not know how to apply it.

Prayer connects us to God's power. When we pray, we invite God into our circumstances. Through prayer, we receive revelation or understanding about what God is doing in our lives.

The quality of revelation we receive often shows us where God is taking us. As stated in *Isaiah 58:14* (NIV), *"Then you will look and be radiant, and your heart will thrill and rejoice, because the abundance of the sea will be brought to you, to you the riches of the nations will come."* When we follow God's ways, we will enjoy the blessings He has for us. There is a special blessing with our names when we align ourselves with God's purpose.

We must pay attention to what God reveals to us to stand tall. In *2 Samuel 23:1-5* (NIV), we see how King David spoke about the importance of following God's direction. God builds a protective wall around those who seek Him earnestly. If we want to know what God thinks about us, we must be alert to His instructions. This means spending time in His Word, listening for His voice, and being open to how He leads us.

Many distractions can distract us from our focus on God. It is essential to seek out things that give us a spiritual advantage. *Proverbs 22:7* (NIV) warns, *"The rich rule over the poor, and the borrower is slave to the lender."* If we do not stand tall in our faith, we can become enslaved by those who have power over us.

Standing tall also requires us to commit to consistency. This means being faithful in our actions, thoughts, and prayers. *Deuteronomy 28:12-13* (NIV) tells us that when we are loyal and obedient to God, we will be the head, not the tail. This means we will be leaders, not followers, in our walk with God.

As we begin this journey of standing tall, remember that our faith is not just for ourselves. It is meant to inspire others and bring glory to God. We are called to be influencers in our communities, sharing the love of Christ and shining our light brightly.

Through this book, we will discover what it means to stand tall, how to harness the power of prayer, and the importance of listening for God's guidance. Together, we will learn how to navigate challenges while remaining faithful to our calling. Let us embrace the journey with courage and faith, knowing God is with us every step.

To embrace a radical mindset means cultivating a way of thinking that is bold, different, and deeply rooted in faith. It involves looking at life from a unique perspective that aligns with God's will rather than conforming to societal norms.

In a society with many demands and distractions to fit in, having a radical mindset empowers us to stand firm in our beliefs and take action that reflects our commitment to God. Radical faith is about more than just believing.

Radical faith is about more than just believing; it is about living out our beliefs in tangible ways. It means stepping out of our comfort zones to follow God's calling. Jesus calls us to be different from the world. In *Matthew 5:14-16* (NIV), *"You are the world's light. A town built on a hill cannot be hidden. Neither do people light a lamp and put it under a bowl. Instead, they put it on its stand, giving everyone in the house light."* This light represents our faith and how we live it out, encouraging others to see God's goodness through us.

We reject the notion of blending in when we embrace a radical mindset. Instead, we seek to stand out for the right reasons. This could mean choosing honesty where others might lie or showing kindness to someone who doesn't deserve it. *Romans 12:2* (NIV) reminds us, *"Do not conform to the pattern of this world but be transformed by renewing your mind. Then you can test and approve*

God's will—*his good, pleasing, and perfect will."* We can change how we think and act by focusing on God's truth.

Being radical often means being willing to stand alone. We might feel called to go another when everyone else goes one way. This can be scary, but it's essential to remember that God is always with us. In *Isaiah 41:10* (NIV), God assures us, *"So do not fear, for I am with you; do not be dismayed, for I am your God. I will strengthen, help, and uphold you with my righteous right hand."* This promise gives us the strength to act boldly, even when we face opposition or criticism.

Consider the story of Daniel in the Bible. Despite the king's decree, he faced great danger for refusing to stop praying to God. Instead of giving in to fear, Daniel remained faithful to his beliefs, demonstrating a radical mindset that inspired others. His courage resulted in God's miraculous protection and a powerful witness to those around him (*Daniel 6:10-23*).

Embracing a radical mindset requires us to live out our values every day. This means making choices that reflect our faith, whether in our relationships, work, or community. Colossians 3:23-24 (NIV) reminds us, *"Whatever you do, do your work heartily, as for the Lord rather than for men, knowing that from the Lord you will receive the inheritance as your reward. You serve the Lord Christ."* This perspective can radically change how we approach our daily tasks and interactions with others.

A radical mindset also challenges us to extend love and grace to those who may not understand our beliefs. We are called to be peacemakers and reflect Christ's love to everyone, even those who oppose us. *Matthew 5:44* (NIV) instructs, *"But I tell you, love your enemies and pray for those who persecute you."* This radical love is not easy, but it sets us apart as followers of Christ.

We must surround ourselves with like-minded individuals as we embrace a radical mindset. Finding a community that encourages and supports our faith can strengthen our resolve. *Hebrews*

10:24-25 (NIV) reminds us, *"And let us consider how we may spur one another on toward love and good deeds, not giving up meeting together, as some are in the habit of doing, but encouraging one another—and all the more as you see the Day approaching."* We can inspire each other to live boldly for God, share our testimonies, and hold each other accountable.

In a world that often pulls us in different directions, embracing a radical mindset means being true to our convictions and supporting others in their journeys. This can create a ripple effect, inspiring others to stand tall in their faith.

Embracing a radical mindset is about more than just thinking differently; it is about transforming our lives to reflect our faith. It challenges us to live boldly, make tough choices, and love others unconditionally.

As we lean into this mindset, we become instruments of change in our lives and the world around us. With God's guidance, we can be the lights that shine in the darkness, demonstrating that a radical life is one filled with purpose, love, and faith. Let us take this journey together, committed to standing tall and embracing the radical love of Christ in all we do.

CHAPTER ONE

THE POWER OF RADICAL FAITH

R adical faith goes beyond simply believing in God; it involves a deep, unwavering trust in His promises and the courage to act on that trust. This faith pushes us to step out of our comfort zones and take risks for God's glory. Radical faith believes that God is capable of the impossible and can work through us to bring about His plans.

Take, for instance, Abraham. He left his home and family, following God's call to an unknown land, believing God would fulfill His promises. His faith was so strong that he was willing to sacrifice his son, Isaac, trusting that God could even raise him from the dead (*Hebrews 11:17-19*, NIV), *"By faith Abraham, when God tested him, offered Isaac as a sacrifice. He who had embraced the promises was about to sacrifice his one and only son, even though God had said to him, 'It is through Isaac that your offspring will be reckoned.' Abraham reasoned that God could even raise the dead, so in a manner of speaking, he received Isaac back from death."* Abraham's story teaches us that radical faith often requires us to relinquish our security and comfort, placing our trust entirely in God's hands.

Another powerful example is the woman's faith with the issue of blood (*Mark 5:25-34*, NIV). She believed she would be healed by touching Jesus' cloak. Her faith drove her to push through a crowd, defying societal norms, to reach Jesus. Her story shows us that radical faith can lead to miraculous outcomes, even in seemingly hopeless situations.

Radical faith isn't just about believing; it's about trusting God so profoundly that it transforms every aspect of our lives. Radical faith draws us closer to God. When we trust Him, especially in complex or uncertain times, we experience His presence and faithfulness in new ways.

We learn to depend on Him for wisdom, provision, and direction, growing more confident in His promises. *Proverbs 3:5-6* (NIV) reminds us, *"Trust in the Lord with all your heart and lean not on your understanding; in all your ways submit to him, and he will make your paths straight."* With radical faith, we approach life's challenges with boldness. Fear and doubt no longer control us because we trust God is with us.

As seen in the story of David and Goliath, when we have faith, even giants fall. Radical faith helps us face difficulties, knowing God's power is more significant than any obstacle. Radical faith doesn't just impact our own lives—it inspires those around us. When people see us stepping out in faith, trusting God for the impossible, they are encouraged to do the same. Our example can give others the courage to leave their comfort zones and pursue God's calling, just as *Hebrews 11* recounts the faith of individuals who inspired generations.

When we walk by radical faith, we become more willing to follow God's lead, even when we don't understand His entire plan. Radical faith reminds us that God sees the bigger picture and that His ways are higher than ours. It empowers us to say "yes" to God, trusting His perfect wisdom over our limited understanding. Abraham's obedience in *Genesis 12* exemplifies trusting God's leading without knowing the final destination.

Living with radical faith creates a lasting impact on those who come after us. It sets a foundation of trust and obedience for future generations to follow.

Our children, family, and community will see the power of faith in action and be encouraged to live their lives for God. As we live with radical faith, we pass on a legacy of wholehearted devotion to Christ, ensuring that faith thrives long after we're gone.

Understanding The Heart Of God

Knowing the heart of God is vital to building a personal relationship with Him. His heart reflects love, compassion, and justice, and He desires us to deeply experience and understand these aspects of His nature. God's nature is love. *1 John 4:8* (NIV), *"Whoever does not love does not know God, because God is love."* His love is not something He does; it's who He is. His unconditional love is not dependent on our behavior or worthiness.

No matter how much we stumble, God's love remains constant. He longs to draw us into a close relationship where we can experience the depth of His affection. Just as a loving parent desires the best for their child, God's love for us is pure, patient, and everlasting. He sent His Son, Jesus, to demonstrate this love most strongly by sacrificing His life for us (*John 3:16*, NIV), *"For God so loved the world that he gave his one and only Son, that whoever believes in him shall not perish but have eternal life."*

God's heart is filled with compassion for those hurting, broken, or in need. *Psalm 34:18* (NIV), *"The Lord is close to the brokenhearted and saves those who are crushed in spirit."* God is not distant or indifferent to our pain. He draws near when we are hurting, offering comfort and healing.

Whether we face grief, disappointment, or sickness, God's compassionate heart moves Him to act on our behalf. In the Gospels, Jesus embodies this compassion: He healed the sick, fed the hungry, and forgave those burdened with sin. His heart breaks for the suffering, and He calls us to show the same care for others.

God's heart is also one of justice. He cares deeply about what is right and fair and calls us to do the same. *Micah 6:8* (NIV), *"He has shown you, O mortal, what is good. And what does the Lord require of you? To act justly, love mercy, and walk humbly with your God."* This means standing up for the oppressed, defending the weak, and ensuring that we live in a way that honors God's standards of righteousness.

God's justice doesn't simply punish wrongdoing—it restores and redeems. Through His justice, He invites us to partner with Him in making the world more aligned with His perfect will, where mercy and fairness reign.

At the center of God's heart is His deep desire for a personal relationship with us. From the moment He created humanity, He intended to live in close fellowship with us, as seen in the Garden of Eden, where He walked and talked with Adam and Eve (*Genesis 3:8*). Despite their disobedience, which broke that perfect fellowship, God never pursued us.

His desire for relationship is evident throughout the Bible, as He sent prophets, gave His commandments, and ultimately sacrificed His Son, Jesus, to restore what was lost. God's love for us is shown through His open invitation to come to Him, no matter our condition. Jesus' words in *Matthew 11:28* (NIV) are a clear example, *"Come to me, all you who are weary and burdened, and I will give you rest."*

This is an invitation not just for the righteous or those who have it all together but for everyone, especially those struggling, tired, and burdened by life. It reveals God's heart and brings us into His presence, where we can find rest and healing for our souls.

He doesn't demand perfection from us before coming to Him; instead, He calls us to go as we are and trust Him to transform us. God doesn't want a distant, surface-level relationship with us. He desires deep, personal intimacy. To understand His heart, we must see that He wants us to know Him, not just about Him.

He wants us to experience His love, hear His voice, and feel His presence daily. *James 4:8* (NIV) says, *"Come near to God, and he will come near to you."* This verse reminds us that God is always ready to meet us, but we also have a part to play in seeking Him.

We grow in intimacy with Him as we draw closer to Him through prayer, worship, and reading His Word. God continually seeks to deepen His connection with us; we find true purpose, peace, and fulfillment in that relationship.

Knowing God intimately changes how we live, think, and interact with others. His love transforms us from the inside out, making us more like Him.

Another profound aspect of God's heart is His unwavering faithfulness. Throughout Scripture and history, God has consistently shown that He keeps His promises, remains true to His Word, and stands by His people, even when we fall short. His faithfulness is essential to His character, assuring us that we can depend on Him in every situation.

The Bible is rich with promises that reveal God's faithfulness. One of the most encouraging reminders in Hebrews 10:23 (NIV) is, *"Let us hold unswervingly to the hope we profess, for He who promised is faithful."* This scripture encourages us to trust in God's promises and to hold onto hope, knowing that God will fulfill what He has said.

Whether it's a promise of provision, peace, guidance, or eternal life, we can be confident that God will do what He has pledged. His faithfulness isn't dependent on our abilities or circumstances but on His perfect character. God's promises are a constant source of hope and strength.

Even when things seem uncertain, we can rest in knowing that God works behind the scenes, orchestrating everything according to His will and timing. Just as He was faithful to Abraham, Moses,

David, and countless others, He remains loyal to us today.

God's unchanging nature provides stability and comfort in a constantly changing world. In *Malachi 3:6* (NIV), God declares, *"I, the Lord, do not change."* This powerful truth means that the same God faithful in the past will remain steadfast in the present and future.

His love, promises, and commitment to us are as steadfast now as they were for the people in biblical times. Because God does not change, we can rely on Him no matter what life brings. While human relationships, circumstances, and emotions may fluctuate, God remains a solid foundation.

His nature ensures that He will always act by His Word, and we can trust Him fully, knowing He is consistently good, just, and merciful.

As we understand God's heart, we are called to reflect His character daily. Our faith should not just be something we profess but live out, embodying His love, compassion, and justice.

Reflecting God's heart means becoming vessels of His grace and truth, living in a way that draws others closer to Him. Jesus commanded us to *"love one another as I have loved you"* (*John 13:34*, NIV). This is one of the most precise expressions of reflecting God's heart.

God's love is unconditional, sacrificial, and patient, and He calls us to love others similarly. This love goes beyond being kind to those who are easy to love—it challenges us to extend love to everyone, including those who are difficult or who may not share our beliefs.

Loving others means being willing to forgive, to be patient, and to serve. It involves stepping outside our comfort zones to meet the needs of those who are hurting, lonely, or in need.

Our love should reflect God's heart—a love that seeks to heal, restore, and bring people closer to Him. God's heart is full of compassion, and He desires for us to mirror this compassion in our interactions with others.

Psalm 103:13 (NIV) reminds us, *"As a father has compassion on his children, so the Lord has compassion on those who fear Him."* This compassion drives us to care for those suffering, empathize with their pain, and offer support.

Showing compassion means being sensitive to the needs of those around us—whether physical, emotional, or spiritual. It might be as simple as offering a listening ear or as significant as providing help to those in crisis.

Just as God reaches out to us in our brokenness, we are called to reach out to others with compassion, understanding, and love.

God's heart also beats for justice. He desires fairness and righteousness and calls us to advocate for the oppressed or marginalized.

Micah 6:8 (NIV) says, *"He has shown you, O mortal, what is good. And what does the Lord require of you? To act justly, to love mercy, and to walk humbly with your God."* Reflecting God's heart means advocating for justice in our communities and beyond.

It means standing up for what is right, speaking out against wrongdoing, and defending those who cannot protect themselves.

Pursuing justice brings the values of God's kingdom—where love, fairness, and mercy reign—into our everyday lives and the world around us.

Going Against The Tide

Going against the tide means standing firm in what you believe, even when everyone around you seems to be going in a different direction. It can be challenging, especially when the world pressures you to change your beliefs and values.

Today's culture can be very loud and persuasive. Everywhere you look—on social media, in movies, and advertising—some messages promote ideas and lifestyles that often contradict the teachings of the Bible.

For example, society often tells us that the most important thing is to be successful and have lots of money. We see ads encouraging us to buy the latest gadgets or the trendiest clothes. This focus on materialism can make us forget what truly matters.

The Bible teaches us the importance of generosity, contentment, and focusing on spiritual wealth instead of earthly things (*Matthew 6:19-21*, NIV), *"Do not store up for yourselves treasures on earth, where moth and rust destroy, and where thieves break in and steal. But store up for yourselves treasures in heaven, where moth and rust do not destroy, and where thieves do not break in and steal. For where your treasure is, there your heart will be also."*

As believers, we need to recognize these pressures and choose to resist them. This might mean saying no to things that don't align with our faith or stepping back from activities that encourage behaviors contrary to God's Word.

It can be challenging, but it is essential to remember that we are called to live differently. Friends and social circles can also significantly impact how we live.

Sometimes, we may feel a strong urge to fit in or avoid conflict with those around us. This can lead us to make choices that don't reflect our true beliefs.

For instance, if our friends are making fun of others, it can be tempting to join in, even if we know it's wrong. Or if everyone is gossiping about someone, we might feel pressured to share in the conversation to avoid being left out.

However, true faith often requires us to refrain from these behaviors. Making choices that honor God can sometimes lead to feelings of isolation or rejection.

But it's important to remember that we are not alone. Many believers face the same challenges. We can draw strength from our faith and find encouragement in God's Word.

Matthew 5:14-16 (NIV) reminds us, *"You are the world's light. A town built on a hill cannot be hidden. Neither do people light a lamp and put it under a bowl. Instead, they put it on its stand, giving everyone in the house light. In the same way, let your light shine before others, that they may see your good deeds and glorify your Father in heaven."*

Noah lived in a world filled with wickedness and corruption. Most people around him had turned away from God and were living in harmful and wrong ways.

However, Noah stood out as a righteous man who followed God. God spoke to Noah and gave him the unusual command to build an ark because He planned to send a flood to cleanse the earth of its evil (*Genesis 6:9-22*).

This task must have seemed absurd to everyone around him. Imagine the ridicule and disbelief he faced as he built a massive boat in the middle of dry land!

Despite the project's mockery and daunting nature, Noah obeyed God. His incredible faith and perseverance saved his family and preserved the animal species for future generations.

Noah's story reminds us that following God's direction, even when it doesn't make sense to others, is a powerful act of faith.

Daniel faced immense pressure to conform to the culture and practices of Babylon when he was taken captive.

The king offered Daniel rich food and wine from his table, which was against God's dietary laws. Rather than give in to the temptation to eat what was forbidden, Daniel courageously chose to stick to his faith.

He requested to eat vegetables and drink water instead (*Daniel*

1:8). This decision was not easy, and Daniel risked being disrespectful or rebellious.

But God honored Daniel's faithfulness. He and his friends looked healthier and more robust than those who ate the king's food.

Later, when a law was made that prohibited praying to anyone but the king, Daniel continued to pray openly to God, even when it meant facing the threat of death (*Daniel 6:10*).

His unwavering commitment saved him and revealed God's glory throughout the kingdom.

Daniel's story encourages us to remain true to our beliefs, even in danger. Shadrach, Meshach, and Abednego were three young men who also faced a significant test of their faith.

When King Nebuchadnezzar built a golden statue and commanded everyone to bow down and worship it, these three refused to do so (*Daniel 3:16-30*, NIV). They were fully aware that their refusal could lead to death in a fiery furnace. In response to the king's threats, they boldly declared, *"We will not serve your gods or worship the image of gold you have set up."* Their faith in God was unshakeable, and they trusted He could save them. Even if He chose not to, they were determined to stand firm.

When thrown into the furnace, they were miraculously unharmed, and a fourth figure, who looked like *"a son of the gods,"* appeared with them (*Daniel 3:25*, NIV). Their courage saved their lives and demonstrated God's power and faithfulness to everyone who witnessed it.

While going against the tide can be challenging, the rewards are profound and transformative. Standing tall for our faith leads to personal growth, deeper intimacy with God, and the opportunity to influence others.

Choosing to go against the tide often leads to significant spiritual growth. Each challenge we face helps strengthen our faith and reliance on God. As we navigate difficulties, we learn to trust Him more, shaping us into the people He has called us to be.

This growth helps us develop patience, perseverance, and a deeper understanding of God's love. Through these experiences, we become more equipped to handle future challenges and to encourage others in their journeys.

Our commitment to standing tall for our faith can significantly influence those around us. When people see our faithfulness and courage, it can inspire them to reflect on their own beliefs and relationship with God.

Matthew 5:16 (NIV) encourages us, *"Let your light shine before others, that they may see your good deeds and glorify your Father in heaven."* By living out our faith boldly, we can draw others closer to God and help them see the beauty of living a life devoted to Him.

Ultimately, our faithfulness to God will be rewarded, not just in this life but in eternity. In *2 Timothy 4:7-8* (NIV), Paul reflects on his life, stating, *"I have fought the good fight, I have finished the course, I have kept the faith. Now there is in store for me the crown of righteousness, which the Lord, the righteous Judge, will award to me on that day—not only to me but also to all who have longed for his appearing."*

This eternal perspective motivates us to persevere despite challenges and remain faithful to God's calling. Knowing that our efforts and sacrifices will be recognized and rewarded in heaven encourages us to keep standing firm in our faith, even when the journey gets tough.

CHAPTER TWO

THE PROCESS OF INFLUENCE

I nfluence is the capacity to affect the character, development, or behavior of someone or something. It can be positive or negative and often happens subtly over time. Christians want our influence to lead others toward Christ and His teachings.

One of the most effective ways to influence others is through our actions. People are more likely to be impacted by what they see us do rather than just what we say. As Paul wrote in *1 Corinthians 11:1* (NIV), *"Follow my example, as I follow the example of Christ."* Our lives should reflect Jesus, drawing others to Him.

The process of influence can be broken down into several stages. Understanding these stages can help us be more effective in our efforts to influence others for Christ.

Influence begins with building genuine relationships. People are likelier to listen to and be influenced by those they trust and care about. Spending time with others, showing interest in their lives, and being a good friend creates a foundation for influence.

In *John 15:12-13* (NIV), Jesus emphasizes the importance of love and friendship, stating, *"My command is this: Love each other as I have loved you. Greater love has no one than this: to lay down one's life for one's friends."*

After establishing relationships, we need to model Christ-like behavior. This includes demonstrating love, kindness, patience, and integrity daily. When people see the fruit of the Spirit in us (*Galatians 5:22-23*, NIV), *"But the fruit of the Spirit is love, joy, peace, forbearance, kindness, goodness, faithfulness, gentleness, and self-control,"* they are more likely to be drawn to our message.

Personal testimonies are powerful tools for influence. Sharing how God has worked in our lives can inspire others and give them hope. Revelation 12:11 (NIV) says, *"They triumphed over him by the blood of the Lamb and by the word of their testimony."* Our stories can serve as a witness to God's faithfulness and grace.

As we influence others, it's essential to encourage and support them in their journey of faith. This may involve praying for them, offering guidance, or simply being there when they need someone to talk to.

Encouragement can significantly impact others, reminding them they are not alone in their struggles.

While the process of influence is rewarding, it also comes with challenges. Not everyone will be open to our influence. Some may be resistant to change or unwilling to accept our beliefs.

It's essential to remain patient and loving, trusting that God can work in their hearts over time. We may fear sharing our faith or standing up for our beliefs will lead to rejection or conflict.

However, *2 Timothy 1:7* (NIV) reminds us, *"For the Spirit God gave us does not make us timid, but gives us power, love and self-discipline."* We can find courage in knowing that God is with us.

In today's fast-paced world, distractions can hinder our ability to influence effectively. It's crucial to remain focused on our purpose and prioritize our relationships with others.

Colossians 3:2 (NIV) encourages us, *"Set your minds on things above, not on earthly things."* Our influence can lead to significant life changes for those around us.

When people encounter the love of Christ through our actions and words, they may decide to follow Him. This ripple effect can transform families, workplaces, and communities.

Our influence can extend beyond our immediate circle. The lives we touch can inspire others to share their faith, creating a legacy of faith that lasts for generations.

Proverbs 22:6 (NIV) emphasizes the importance of training children correctly: *"Start children off on the way they should go, and even when they are old, they will not turn from it."*

The Path To Greatness: A Threefold Approach

Greatness is often seen as an extraordinary achievement or a significant societal contribution. However, true greatness is more than just accolades or success; it is rooted in character, purpose, and our impact on others.

As believers, we are called to pursue greatness that aligns with God's will and reflects His love and truth. Greatness can be defined as living a life that glorifies God and serves others.

It's about making a difference in our communities, families, and workplaces by embodying the values of the Kingdom of God.

In Matthew 20:26-28, Jesus teaches that *"Whoever wants to become great among you must be your servant, and whoever wants to be first must be your slave—just as the Son of Man did not come to be served, but to serve, and to give his life as a ransom for many"* (NIV).

To walk the path to greatness, we must first understand our purpose. Each person is created with unique gifts and a specific calling.

We find fulfillment and direction when we align our lives with God's purpose.

Jeremiah 29:11 reminds us, *"For I know the plans I have for you,"* declares the Lord, "plans to prosper you and not to harm you, plans to give you hope and a future" (NIV).

The Threefold Approach To Greatness

The path to greatness can be approached through Character Development, Service to Others, and Continuous Growth. Each principle plays a crucial role in shaping a life of true greatness.

Character Development

Character development is essential for achieving greatness in our lives. It shapes who we are and how we interact with the world.

Integrity is the bedrock of solid character. It includes our values, principles, and daily choices.

When we have integrity, we are honest and consistent in our actions, which builds trust with others.

"The integrity of the upright guides them" (Proverbs 11:3, NIV). Our moral compass helps us make wise decisions when we act with integrity.

It encourages us to live out our faith daily, even when faced with challenges.

Always choose honesty, even when it's complicated. Align our actions with our beliefs and principles.

Let our words match our actions, demonstrating reliability and trustworthiness.

Humility is crucial for true greatness. It helps us recognize our dependence on God and teaches us to value others above ourselves.

"Do nothing out of selfish ambition or vain conceit, but in humility consider others better than yourselves" (Philippians 2:3, NIV).

This attitude fosters healthy relationships and creates a

supportive community.

Take time to listen to others' opinions and feelings.

Recognize that we don't have all the answers and need God and others to succeed.

The path to greatness will inevitably include challenges and setbacks.

Resilience is the ability to bounce back from difficulties and keep moving forward despite obstacles.

"Suffering produces perseverance; perseverance, character; and character, hope" (Romans 5:3-4, NIV).

View difficulties as opportunities for growth rather than setbacks.

Surround ourselves with supportive friends and family who can encourage us during tough times.

Focus on the positives in our lives, which can help shift our perspective during challenging moments.

Service to Others

Service to others is a vital aspect of living a life of greatness.

It reflects our commitment to Christ and embodies love, community, and leadership principles.

Greatness is found in serving others, and Jesus perfectly modeled this during His time on Earth.

In John 13:1-17, Jesus washed His disciples' feet, demonstrating humility and love.

This act showed that authentic leadership involves serving others regardless of status.

We should look for ways to help those around us through acts of kindness, support, or presence.

Encourage others in their endeavors, offering guidance and

assistance to help them reach their potential.

When we serve selflessly, we reflect Christ's love and positively impact our communities.

Serving others helps create a sense of community.

When we come together to support one another, we build connections that strengthen our relationships.

"Spur one another toward love and good deeds" (Hebrews 10:24-25, NIV).

Engage in community service projects, volunteer at local shelters, or host events that unite people.

Make an effort to know your neighbors and coworkers.

Small acts of kindness can go a long way in building relationships.

We naturally take on leadership roles in our communities as we serve others.

Leadership is not merely about titles; it's about influence and the example we set for others. *"Let your light shine before others, that they may see your good deeds and glorify your Father in heaven."* (Matthew 5:16).

When we act with kindness and service, we inspire others to do the same. To show our commitment to serving others, we regularly participate in community service or church activities. We invite friends and family to join us in serving, sharing our experiences, and highlighting the joys of giving back.

Continuous Growth

Greatness involves a commitment to lifelong learning. Seeking knowledge helps us grow personally and spiritually.

Proverbs 1:5 says, *"Let the wise listen and add to their learning"* (NIV). This encourages us to be open to new ideas and insights that can enrich our lives.

Read books, articles, and resources that challenge and inspire you. Whether it's scripture, biographies of great leaders, or books on personal development, each piece of knowledge contributes to your growth. Participate in educational opportunities at church, community centers, or online. These experiences can deepen your understanding of various subjects and help you grow in your ability to serve others.

When we continually seek knowledge, we make informed decisions and improve our skills. This growth enables us to serve others more effectively and with a more significant impact.

James 1:5, *"If any of you lacks wisdom, you should ask God, who gives generously to all without finding fault, and it will be given to you"* (NIV). This encourages us to seek God's wisdom in every aspect.

By seeking God's guidance, we ensure our growth is meaningful and aligned with His purpose for our lives. Growth often involves change, which can be uncomfortable but is essential for development.

2 Corinthians 5:17, *"Therefore, if anyone is in Christ, the new creation has come: The old has gone, the new is here!"* (NIV). This verse emphasizes that God transforms us into new beings involving change.

Open yourself to opportunities that broaden your horizon. This might involve trying new activities, meeting new people, or stepping into leadership roles. Consider how far you've come and what changes have positively impacted your growth.

Celebrate your progress and remain open to the changes that God may bring. Embracing change allows us to evolve and adapt, making us more resilient in our pursuit of greatness. Change often leads to new perspectives and opportunities that can enhance our journey.

The Rewards Of Greatness

Walking the path to greatness through character development, service to others, and continuous growth brings numerous rewards. These rewards not only enrich our own lives but also benefit those around us.

Fulfillment:

True greatness leads to a profound sense of fulfillment from living a life aligned with God's purpose. This fulfillment is not just about personal achievements; it encompasses a more profound joy and satisfaction that arises when we engage in meaningful actions that reflect our faith.

We begin seeing value in our lives when we understand our unique purpose. Embracing this purpose gives us direction and clarity, guiding our decisions and actions.

Living in line with our purpose brings joy that can only come from knowing we are fulfilling our God-given calling. In the everyday moments, big or small, we see how our actions align with His will.

Recognizing that our lives contribute to something larger than ourselves instills a sense of meaning. Whether through serving others, sharing the Gospel, or fostering community, we see how our efforts play a role in God's grand design.

Fulfillment often arises from the knowledge that we are making a difference in the lives of those around us. Our kindness, support, and encouragement can profoundly affect others, creating community positivity.

Simple acts of kindness—whether volunteering, lending a listening ear, or providing help in need—can lead to meaningful connections.

These interactions create bonds and foster a sense of belonging, leading to lasting joy. Being a mentor or a supportive friend can bring fulfillment. When we invest time and energy into helping others grow, we enrich their lives and experience a more profound sense of purpose.

When our lives are aligned with God's purpose, we discover fulfillment that transcends worldly achievements. This alignment helps us focus on what truly matters and enables us to find joy in our daily lives.

As we reflect God's love and grace in our interactions, we become living testimonies of His goodness. Our lives exemplify His transformative power, encouraging others to seek Him.

Understanding that our efforts are part of God's plan encourages us to persevere. Our fulfillment is rooted in the knowledge that our lives can have a lasting impact in this world and beyond.

Positive Impact:

When we consistently live with integrity and a clear purpose, we set an example for others. People are drawn to those who embody values they admire, and our commitment to these principles encourages them to adopt similar attitudes.

As we demonstrate kindness, compassion, and service, we help cultivate an environment where these qualities are celebrated.

This culture of greatness motivates others to act with the same integrity and purpose, creating a cycle of inspiration and positivity. By inspiring others, we empower them to make positive changes in their own lives.

Our actions can encourage someone to step out of their comfort zone, take on new challenges, or extend kindness to others. When we serve and uplift one another, we create a community that nurtures growth. People feel valued and supported, leading to an environment where they can thrive and contribute their unique gifts.

As others witness our dedication to greatness, they become

motivated to join and contribute to the cause. This collective effort strengthens community bonds and enhances the overall impact we can make together.

Serving alongside others fosters strong relationships. These connections create a sense of belonging, empower individuals to share their challenges and triumphs, and further enrich the community.

When we live out our faith through good deeds and a servant's heart, we testify to God's love and grace. This testimony can lead others to seek a relationship with Him, recognizing the source of our greatness. Our positive impact can inspire others to explore their faith journeys. By living authentically and serving selflessly, we demonstrate the transformative power of God's love, inviting others to experience it for themselves.

A Lasting Legacy

By embodying faith, service, and continuous growth, we provide an excellent example for others. Our daily actions, decisions, and attitudes reflect our cherished values, influencing how future generations approach their lives.

When we prioritize our faith and serve others selflessly, we teach future generations the importance of these qualities. They learn that greatness is found in personal achievement and our impact on others' lives.

Our commitment to service can inspire a culture where helping others is valued. When the next generation sees us actively engaging in acts of kindness, they are likelier to adopt similar attitudes and behaviors.

As the Bible reminds us, *"A good person leaves an inheritance for their children's children"* (Proverbs 13:22, NIV). This inheritance goes beyond financial resources; it encompasses the values and principles we pass down.

Our legacy is one of character, integrity, and a commitment

to serving others. These qualities shape how our children and grandchildren navigate their lives, influencing their choices and relationships.

By demonstrating resilience in the face of challenges, we teach future generations to face their obstacles with courage. Our examples of perseverance can encourage them to keep striving for their goals, even in difficult times.

As we pave the way for others to follow, we can nurture the next generation of leaders. By recognizing and encouraging their talents, we help them grow into individuals who can significantly impact the world.

Our commitment to service and integrity can instill values in future leaders. They learn that authentic leadership is about serving others, making decisions grounded in moral principles, and creating positive change in their communities.

By investing in the development of future leaders, we contribute to a brighter future for our families, communities, and the world. The legacy of greatness we leave behind can inspire and empower the next generation to pursue their paths of significance.

This legacy inspires and empowers future generations to make a lasting impact. Living a life of faith, service, and growth creates a lasting legacy that transcends our lifetime.

CHAPTER THREE

THE NECESSITY
OF PRAYER

Prayer is the primary way we communicate with God. Just as we need to talk with friends and family to maintain our relationships, we need to converse with God to grow closer to Him.

In (James 4:8, NIV), *"Draw near to God and He will draw near to you,"* we are encouraged to cultivate a deeper relationship with God through prayer. This relationship is built through open and honest dialogue.

Prayer allows us to express our thoughts, feelings, and concerns to God. *"Do not be anxious about anything, but in every situation, by prayer and petition, with thanksgiving, present your requests to God"* (Philippians 4:6-7, NIV). When we bring our worries and joys before Him, we invite His presence into our lives, making our relationship more personal and meaningful.

In times of uncertainty, prayer is crucial for seeking guidance. *"Trust in the Lord with all your heart and lean not on your understanding"* (Proverbs 3:5-6, NIV). When we pray for wisdom, we acknowledge our need for God's insight and guidance in making decisions.

Through prayer, we can seek to understand God's will for our lives.

"Do not conform to the pattern of this world, but be transformed by the renewing of your mind. Then you will be able to test and approve what God's will is—his good, pleasing, and perfect will" (Romans 12:2, NIV). Prayer helps us align our desires with God's plans, allowing us to walk in His purpose.

Prayer brings peace during difficult times. *"Peace I leave with you; my peace I give you. I do not give to you as the world gives"* (John 14:27, NIV). When we turn to prayer in times of trouble, we can find comfort in God's presence.

"The Spirit helps us in our weakness. We do not know what we ought to pray for, but the Spirit himself intercedes for us through wordless groans" (Romans 8:26, NIV). When we feel overwhelmed, prayer allows us to surrender our struggles to God and receive the strength we need to endure.

Prayer is a way to express our gratitude to God for His blessings. *"Be joyful always; pray continually; give thanks in all circumstances"* (1 Thessalonians 5:16-18, NIV). When we regularly thank God in prayer, we cultivate a heart of gratitude.

Prayer is also a means of worship. *"Enter his gates with thanksgiving and his courts with praise"* (Psalm 100:4, NIV). We align our hearts with His truth by praising God for who He is and what He has done.

Prayer is essential for interceding on behalf of others. *"I urge, then, first of all, that petitions, prayers, intercession, and thanksgiving be made for all people—for kings and all those in authority"* (1 Timothy 2:1-2, NIV). When we pray for others, we participate in God's work in their lives.

"The prayer of a righteous person is powerful and effective" (James 5:16, NIV). When we lift each other in prayer, we strengthen our bonds and encourage one another in faith.

Prayer strengthens our faith as we witness God's answers and provision. *"If any of you lacks wisdom, you should ask God, who gives generously to all without finding fault, and it will be given to you"* (James 1:5, NIV). Each answered prayer builds our trust and deepens our reliance on Him.

As we pray, we experience God's presence in our lives. *"The Lord is near to all who call on him"* (Psalm 145:18, NIV). This closeness fosters a deeper relationship with God.

Prayer As Our Sustaining Power

Prayer is not just a ritual or a routine; it is a powerful lifeline that sustains us in our daily walk with God. In times of joy and sorrow, success and failure, prayer is a source of strength that empowers us to face life's challenges. Understanding the sustaining power of prayer can transform our faith journey and help us rely on God more fully.

In times of weakness or despair, prayer becomes our lifeline to God's strength. *"He gives strength to the weary and increases the power of the weak"* (Isaiah 40:29, NIV). When we feel overwhelmed, turning to God in prayer allows us to draw upon His divine strength, enabling us to persevere even when we feel like giving up.

Through prayer, we find restoration and renewal for our spirits. In these moments of communion with God, we are reminded of His unwavering support and love. As we lay our burdens before Him, we exchange our weaknesses for His strength, discovering a renewed sense of hope and purpose.

Prayer connects us to God and invites the Holy Spirit to work within us. *"Strengthened with power through His Spirit in our inner being"* (Ephesians 3:16, NIV). This divine empowerment equips us to face challenges with courage and resilience.

As we pray, we open our hearts to the Holy Spirit's guidance, allowing Him to guide our decisions and actions. The Spirit provides comfort and assurance during difficult times, reminding us that we are not alone in our struggles.

This connection with the Holy Spirit helps us to remain steadfast in our faith and inspires us to act according to God's will. Through the empowerment of the Holy Spirit, we gain the boldness to step out in faith and take action in our lives. Prayer ignites a fire within us, encouraging us to pursue our God-given purpose with confidence and strength.

During stressful and anxious moments, prayer serves as a haven where we can unload our burdens. *"Do not be anxious about anything, but in every situation, by prayer and petition, with thanksgiving, present your requests to God"* (Philippians 4:6-7, NIV).

When we pray and bring our worries to Him, we experience a divine exchange: our anxiety is replaced with His peace, which guards our hearts and minds. This peace, beyond understanding, provides reassurance that God is in control, allowing us to face our circumstances confidently.

In prayer, we practice surrendering our worries to God. This act of releasing our concerns allows us to trust Him more fully. We find a profound sense of relief and peace when we let go of our need to control outcomes and place our faith in His goodness.

Prayer opens the door to experiencing God's comforting presence. *"The Lord is close to the brokenhearted"* (Psalm 34:18, NIV). When we turn to Him in prayer, we encounter His nearness, which provides comfort and reassurance, especially during our most challenging moments.

In prayer, we find comfort and healing in our hearts. God meets us in our pain and offers His loving embrace, reminding us that we are never alone.

This assurance fosters an environment where we can process our feelings and solace in His presence. Through prayer, we gain a renewed perspective and hope in turbulent times.

We often find clarity and wisdom to navigate our challenges as we pour our hearts into God. This hope helps us to remain anchored in faith, even when circumstances seem overwhelming.

When faced with important decisions, prayer becomes our first step in seeking wisdom. *"If any of you lacks wisdom, you should ask God, who gives generously to all without finding fault, and it will be given to you"* (James 1:5, NIV).

We invite His perspective into our decision-making process by bringing our uncertainties to God in prayer. This divine wisdom allows us to see beyond immediate circumstances and understand the broader implications of our choices.

We may not always receive immediate answers as we pray, but we gain clarity and peace about the following steps. Prayer helps us slow down and contemplate our decisions, guiding us away from impulsive actions.

In this way, prayer nurtures a deeper relationship with God, allowing us to trust His timing and guidance. Through prayer, we can align our desires with God's life purpose.

"Delight yourself in the Lord, and he will give you the desires of your heart" (Psalm 37:4, NIV). This verse highlights the importance of focusing our hearts on God, seeking to understand His will, and finding joy in His presence.

As we grow closer to Him through prayer, our desires naturally shift toward what is good, right, and fulfilling in His sight. In worship, we also allow God to shape our hearts and minds, refining our desires to reflect His values. This transformation helps us prioritize what truly matters and equips us to make decisions that honor Him.

When our hearts are aligned with God's will, we find peace and assurance in our choices, knowing we are walking the path He has set before us. Ultimately, prayer leads us toward fulfilling and purposeful lives. When we seek God's wisdom and align our desires with His, we can confidently navigate our decisions, knowing we are being led by His hand.

One of the most potent aspects of prayer is witnessing God's faithfulness in our lives. When we pray and see God's answers—yes, no, or wait—we gain firsthand experience of His presence and involvement. *"This is the confidence we have in approaching God: that if we ask anything according to his will, he hears us"* (1 John 5:14, NIV).

Each answered prayer reminds us of His constant care and attention to our needs, reinforcing our trust in Him. Reflecting on past prayers and how God has responded to them in challenging times strengthens our faith.

Regular prayer fosters a habit of trust in God. *"Faith comes from hearing, and hearing through the word of Christ"* (Romans 10:17, NIV). Prayer and Scripture reading deepen our understanding of God's character and promises.

As we engage with His Word and bring our thoughts and questions to Him in prayer, we cultivate a robust faith that withstands life's challenges. Over time, this habit of worship transforms our perspective.

We learn to trust God for our immediate needs and His overarching plan. The more we pray, the more we recognize His faithfulness and guidance, strengthening our faith.

Just as our bodies require nourishment to thrive, our spirits need the sustenance of prayer for renewal. Jesus extends an open invitation, *"Come to me, all you who are weary and burdened, and I will give you rest"* (Matthew 11:28-30, NIV).

In the quiet moments of prayer, we can lay down our burdens and find refreshment for our weary souls. This connection with God rejuvenates us, providing the strength and peace we need to face each day.

"Set your minds on things above, not earthly things" (Colossians 3:2,

NIV). In prayer, we consciously redirect our thoughts from our problems to God's greatness.

When we bring our concerns to God in prayer, we gain a clearer perspective on our situations. Rather than being consumed by our struggles, we find peace knowing God is in control.

Regularly renewing our spirits through prayer, we become better equipped to handle life's ups and downs.

Unlocking The Miraculous Through Prayer

When we pray, we actively seek God's guidance and wisdom. Proverbs 3:5- 6 encourages us to trust in the Lord with all our hearts and not lean on our understanding. By acknowledging Him in all our ways, we open ourselves to His miraculous plans for us. Prayer allows us to pause, listen, and discern His voice amidst the noise of life, helping us navigate our paths with clarity and purpose.

We express our desires and concerns in prayer, inviting God to direct our steps. As we submit our plans to Him, we see how His guidance can lead us to opportunities and paths we might not have considered. This practice helps us to remain flexible and open-hearted, ready to follow where He leads.

Prayer is an act of humility, recognizing that God's plans and wisdom surpass our own. When we approach Him with a willing heart, we admit we do not have all the answers. This humility allows us to be receptive to His guidance and prompts us to trust His sovereignty.

"Your kingdom come, you will be done" (Matthew 6:10, NIV). This aspect of prayer is crucial as it encourages us to align our desires with His purposes. By submitting our will to God, we create a space for Him to work miracles in our lives.

We may not always understand His ways, but through prayer, we can rest assured that *"God works all things together for the good of those who love him"* (Romans 8:28, NIV). We may find our hearts transformed as we pray for God's will.

When we pray, we are not simply speaking words into the air; we are communicating directly with the Creator of the universe. Our prayers are powerful because they connect us with God's authority and sovereignty.

"The prayer of a righteous person is powerful and effective" (James 5:16, NIV). When we pray with sincerity and faith, we invite God to intervene in our circumstances, bringing about change that only He can achieve.

Jesus encourages us to pray with confidence and faith, knowing God listens to our requests. *"Whatever you ask in my name, I will do it"* (John 14:13-14, NIV). This assurance reminds us that God is not distant or unwilling to intervene.

Prayer becomes a powerful tool when we connect it with God's promises in Scripture. *"Faith comes from hearing, and hearing through the word of Christ"* (Romans 10:17, NIV). As we pray and meditate on God's Word, our faith deepens, and we become more confident in His ability to perform miracles.

"For no matter how many promises God has made, they are 'Yes' in Christ" (2 Corinthians 1:20, NIV). This powerful truth reminds us that God is consistent and faithful in His promises.

Jesus emphasizes the importance of persistence in prayer through the parable of the persistent widow in Luke 18:1-8. The widow's unwavering persistence eventually leads the judge to grant her request, showing us that continuous and faithful prayer can bring divine intervention.

"Do not be anxious about anything, but in every situation, by prayer and petition, with thanksgiving, present your requests to God" (Philippians 4:6-7, NIV). As we pray, God provides the peace

we need to trust in Him, even when the answer is unclear.

The Role Of Revelation In Our Lives

Revelation plays a vital role in our spiritual journey, helping us understand who God is and His character. Through Scripture, prayer, and personal experiences, we gain valuable insights into God's love, grace, and faithfulness.

"In the beginning was the Word, and the Word was with God, and the Word was God" (John 1:1, NIV). This passage of scriptures shows us how we deepen our relationship with Him, allowing us to know Him personally and intimately. God's revelation provides clarity about His will for our lives.

In Jeremiah 29:11, God assures us, *"For I know the plans I have for you," declares the Lord, "plans to prosper you and not to harm you, plans to give you hope and a future"* (NIV). When we seek revelation through prayer and Scripture, we receive guidance on our choices, helping us align our lives with His purpose.

Revelation is essential for nurturing and growing our faith. *"Consequently, faith comes from hearing the message, and the message is heard through the word about Christ"* (Romans 10:17, NIV).

Regularly engaging with God's Word helps us develop a stronger foundation for our beliefs and encourages us during challenging times.

Revelation also plays a crucial role in transforming our minds and hearts. *"Do not conform to the pattern of this world, but be transformed by the renewing of your mind"* (Romans 12:2, NIV). God's Word reveals truth, enabling us to see the world through His lens rather than our own.

Revelation acts as a compass, guiding us in our decisions and actions. *"Trust in the Lord with all your heart and lean not on your understanding; in all your ways submit to him, and he will make your paths straight"* (Proverbs 3:5-6, NIV). We gain insight into the best course of action for various situations by seeking God's revelation.

Through revelation, we gain an understanding of our purpose in life. *"For we are God's handiwork, created in Christ Jesus to do good works, which God prepared in advance for us to do"* (Ephesians 2:10, NIV). Revelation helps us discover our unique gifts and how to use them for His glory and the benefit of others.

Revelation fosters unity within the body of Christ. *"Make every effort to keep the unity of the Spirit through the bond of peace"* (Ephesians 4:3, NIV). When we share insights and revelations, we build each other up and strengthen our relationships as fellow believers.

Revelation can serve as a source of encouragement and support in our relationships. Sharing what God has revealed can uplift and inspire others in their journeys.

Revelation empowers us to share God's truth with others. *"Go and make disciples of all nations, baptizing them in the name of the Father and the Son and the Holy Spirit, and teaching them to obey everything I have commanded you"* (Matthew 28:19-20, NIV).

Revelation helps us live as lights in a dark world. *"You are the light of the world. A town built on a hill cannot be hidden. Neither do people light a lamp and put it under a bowl. Instead, they put it on its stand, and it gives light to everyone in the house"* (Matthew 5:14-15, NIV).

CHAPTER FOUR

THE STRENGTH OF COMMUNITY

A community rooted in shared faith provides a foundation for understanding and practicing beliefs. Members with similar values can encourage others to live out those principles daily. This shared faith helps foster unity and strengthens the bond among members.

Gathering together for worship magnifies the experience of faith. *"Let us consider how we may spur one another on toward love and good deeds, not giving up meeting together, as some are in the habit of doing, but encouraging one another—and all the more as you see the Day approaching"* (Hebrews 10:24-25, NIV). Worshiping together creates a powerful atmosphere where individuals can connect with God and each other.

In challenging times, a community offers emotional support and encouragement. *"Carry each other's burdens"* (Galatians 6:2, NIV) reflects the heart of community care. When we share our struggles, we lighten our load and remind one another that we are not alone.

A strong community can provide practical assistance in times of need. Whether through meal trains, financial support, or helping with chores, tangible acts of service demonstrate love and compassion, reinforcing the community's strength.

Being part of a community helps us stay accountable in our spiritual journey. *"As iron sharpens iron, so one person sharpens another"* (Proverbs 27:17, NIV). Community members can challenge and inspire one another to deepen their relationship with God.

Communities often provide opportunities for learning and growth through Bible studies, discussions, and workshops. These gatherings create spaces for sharing knowledge and experiences, fostering spiritual maturity among members.

Encouragement is a vital aspect of community life. *"Therefore encourage one another and build each other up"* (1 Thessalonians 5:11, NIV). Positive reinforcement from fellow believers can motivate us to pursue our goals and deepen our faith.

Communities often consist of individuals from diverse backgrounds, cultures, and experiences. This diversity enriches the community, offering a variety of perspectives and insights. *"Just as a body, though one, has many parts, but all its many parts form one body, so it is with Christ"* (1 Corinthians 12:12, NIV).

A strong community embraces inclusion, welcoming everyone regardless of background or circumstances. This openness creates a safe space for individuals to express their faith and share their stories without fear of judgment.

Being part of a community gives individuals a sense of purpose. Members can work together to make a difference in their neighborhoods and beyond when united around a joint mission. *"Go and make disciples of all nations, baptizing them in the name of the Father and the Son and the Holy Spirit, and teaching them to obey everything I have commanded you"* (Matthew 28:19-20, NIV).

A strong community often engages in outreach efforts, serving those in need. Acts of kindness, volunteering, and mission work are expressions of faith in action that benefit others and strengthen the bonds among community members.

Community fosters friendships and fellowship, providing a space where individuals can connect on a deeper level. Shared experiences, laughter, and support create lasting bonds that enrich our lives.

Building Relationships That Empower

Relationships provide a safety net in difficult times. Having people around you who genuinely care can make a significant difference when facing challenges. *"Two are better than one because they have a good return for their labor: If either of them falls, one can help the other up"* (Ecclesiastes 4:9-10, NIV) emphasizes the importance of companionship.

Empowering relationships promotes mutual growth. When we surround ourselves with people who inspire and uplift us, we are more likely to strive for excellence and push through obstacles. *"As iron sharpens iron, so one person sharpens another"* (Proverbs 27:17, NIV) reminds us of the value of constructive relationships.

Trust is the foundation of any strong relationship. Being honest, reliable, and transparent helps foster an environment where individuals feel safe to share their thoughts and feelings. *"A gossip betrays a confidence, but a trustworthy person keeps a secret"* (Proverbs 11:13, NIV).

Creating a culture of openness allows for authentic conversations. When people feel free to express themselves without fear of judgment, it strengthens the bond between them. Active listening involves fully engaging with the speaker, paying attention to their words, and seeking to understand their perspective. *"My dear brothers and sisters, take note of this: Everyone should be quick to listen, slow to speak, and slow to become angry"* (James 1:19, NIV).

When we listen actively, we can respond with empathy

EXTRAORDINARY ACHIEVEMENTS

and compassion. Understanding others' feelings helps build a supportive environment where everyone feels valued. Empathy nurtures trust and strengthens relationships.

Healthy boundaries are crucial in empowering relationships. They ensure that both parties respect each other's needs and limits. Setting boundaries helps prevent misunderstandings and promotes a healthy balance in relationships. *"Speaking the truth in love, we will grow to become in every respect the mature body of him who is the head, that is, Christ"* (Ephesians 4:15, NIV).

Empowering relationships involves holding each other accountable for personal growth and commitments. This accountability can encourage individuals to stay focused on their goals and follow their promises. *"Wounds from a friend can be trusted, but an enemy multiplies kisses"* (Proverbs 27:6, NIV).

In an empowering relationship, both parties encourage each other to take responsibility for their actions. Practicing forgiveness allows individuals to move past hurts and grow stronger together. *"Bear with each other and forgive one another if any of you has a grievance against someone. Forgive as the Lord forgave you"* (Colossians 3:13, NIV).

Extending grace to one another creates a nurturing environment where individuals feel accepted and supported. Building empowering relationships requires time and effort. Regularly spending quality time together strengthens bonds and deepens connections.

The Importance of Collective Prayer

Collective prayer fosters a sense of unity among believers. When people come together to pray, they share their burdens, joys, and hopes, creating a solid bond and helping individuals feel connected.

In Acts 2:42, the early church devoted themselves to prayer and fellowship, strengthening their community. Praying together provides encouragement and support, demonstrating love and compassion.

"Carry each other's burdens; in this way, you will fulfill the law of Christ" (Galatians 6:2, NIV) reminds us of the importance of mediation. There is power in collective prayer when believers come together in agreement. *"Again, truly I tell you that if two of you on earth agree about anything they ask for, it will be done for them by my Father in heaven"* (Matthew 18:19-20, NIV).

Collective prayer allows individuals to share the burden of their concerns. Knowing others pray for the same issues can lighten the load and bring comfort. *"Do not be anxious about anything, but in every situation, by prayer and petition, with thanksgiving, present your requests to God"* (Philippians 4:6, NIV).

In a group prayer setting, individuals can learn from one another's experiences and insights. Hearing different perspectives deepens one's understanding of God and strengthens faith. *"As iron sharpens iron, so one person sharpens another"* (Proverbs 27:17, NIV).

Collective prayer promotes a culture of worship within a community. Regular gatherings inspire others to join in and develop their prayer lives, strengthening the community spiritually.

Collective prayer allows individuals to intercede for others. *"I looked for someone to stand in the gap and stand before me on behalf of the land so I would not have to destroy it, but I found no one"* (Ezekiel 22:30, NIV), highlighting the importance of standing in the gap.

When believers gather to pray, they often experience God's presence. This shared spiritual experience leads to deep worship and greater awareness of God's work. *"How good and pleasant it is when God's people live together in unity!"* (Psalm 133:1, NIV).

Collective prayer often leads to spontaneous worship and

thanksgiving. Sharing testimonies and praise reports fills the atmosphere with gratitude, drawing everyone closer to God.

When facing important decisions, collective prayer provides a platform for seeking God's guidance. *"If any of you lacks wisdom, you should ask God, who gives generously to all without finding fault"* (James 1:5, NIV).

Praying together helps align hearts with God's will for the community. When people come together, they better understand His purposes and plans, leading to collective action and service.

Communities that prioritize collective prayer set an example for future generations. *"We will not hide these truths from our children; we will tell the next generation about the glorious deeds of the Lord, his power, and his mighty wonders"* (Psalm 78:4, NIV).

A community that values collective prayer becomes a robust and faithful body of believers, resilient in facing challenges and supporting overall spiritual health.

CHAPTER FIVE

CONSISTENCY: THE KEY TO MASTERY

Consistency allows us to practice regularly, turning actions into habits. When we commit to a routine, our minds and bodies adapt, making it easier to perform tasks automatically. As the saying goes, "Practice makes perfect." Whether learning a musical instrument or mastering a sport, daily practice is crucial for progress.

Consistency helps us push through moments of resistance by establishing a rhythm in our activities. By sticking to our plans, we learn to overcome challenges and keep moving forward. Mastery is rarely achieved overnight; it requires small, incremental steps taken consistently over time.

As a seed grows into a mighty tree, our skills and knowledge develop through persistent effort. Each small achievement builds on the last, leading to significant progress. With consistency, we can track our growth over time. Regular evaluation of our performance helps identify areas for improvement and celebrate achievements.

Consistency teaches us to stay committed, even when faced with setbacks. Every journey has its ups and downs, but those who remain consistent are better equipped to weather the storms. Resilience builds character and strengthens resolve.

Inconsistency can lead to frustration and confusion, but a consistent approach encourages learning from mistakes. Instead of giving up, we analyze what went wrong, make adjustments, and continue on our path to mastery.

Consistency requires setting clear, achievable goals. When we have a clear vision, we focus efforts on necessary steps. This focus eliminates distractions and keeps us on track. Consistent practice promotes mindfulness of our actions and a deeper understanding of our skills.

Consistency demands self-discipline, commitment to regular practice, goal prioritization, and effective time management. This discipline enhances overall productivity. Establishing routines automates actions, making it easier to stay committed.

As we practice consistently, we build trust in our abilities and confidence in our ability to take on new challenges. Consistent practice also opens the door to feedback from mentors, peers, and self-assessment. Constructive criticism refines skills and reinforces confidence.

When we demonstrate consistency in our actions, we inspire others. Our dedication motivates others to pursue their goals, creating a ripple effect of positive change. Mastery achieved through consistency leaves a lasting impact, inspiring future generations.

The Art Of Being A Finisher

Since our world is filled with distractions and endless tasks, finishing what we started is a valuable skill. This art leads to personal satisfaction and contributes to success in various aspects of life. Completing tasks provides a sense of achievement, building confidence and self-worth.

Finishing tasks develop consistency and perseverance and

demonstrates responsibility and dedication. It also sets an example for others and showcases dependability. Completing tasks builds discipline, trains us to overcome obstacles, and fosters trust in relationships.

Overcoming Procrastination

Procrastination can stem from fear, feeling overwhelmed, or lacking interest. Recognizing triggers helps address them directly. Understanding the reasons behind procrastination enables the creation of personalized strategies.

Breaking tasks into smaller steps and focusing on progress rather than perfection overcomes procrastination.

Cultivating a Finisher's Mindset

A finisher's mindset prioritizes completion, persistence, and goal achievement. Setting clear goals, breaking them down into smaller steps, and writing them down helps track progress and stay motivated.

Visualization activates motivation and provides satisfaction. Regularly revisiting the image of success reignites drive and determination.

Additional Strategies

A daily routine provides structure and allocates time for tasks. Consistency strengthens commitment, and minimizing distractions enhances focus.

Embracing the journey maintains motivation and finds fulfillment in the process. Celebrating minor achievements builds momentum.

A robust support system, including accountability partners and mentors, provides motivation and guidance. Completing tasks opens doors to new opportunities, and evaluating and setting new goals creates a cycle of growth and achievement.

Discipline and Focus: Key to Finishing Strong

Discipline and focus are critical components of being a finisher. By creating habits and environments that support your goals, you can significantly increase your chances of completing tasks and achieving success. A daily routine provides a framework for your day, allowing you to allocate time for tasks that must be completed. With a routine, you can plan your day around what needs to get done, making it easier to focus on one task at a time without feeling overwhelmed.

Over time, following a routine can become second nature, reinforcing discipline and making finishing tasks a regular part of your life. Consistency is the foundation of discipline. When you regularly stick to your routine, it strengthens your commitment to completing assignments. Even on days when motivation wanes, the routine can keep you on track, ensuring that you still make progress.

Distractions can quickly derail focus and prevent you from finishing tasks. Whether it's your phone, social media, or background noise, it's essential to identify the distractions that most commonly interrupt your focus. Once you recognize them, you can take steps to reduce or eliminate their influence.

Setting up an environment that supports concentration is critical for staying focused. This might mean working in a quiet room, turning off notifications on your devices, or using tools like noise-canceling headphones. By proactively creating a space where distractions are minimized, you enhance your ability to focus, helping you complete tasks more efficiently.

Embracing The Journey

Success is defined not only by the result but also by the growth and experiences gained along the way. Embracing the journey allows us to maintain motivation, learn from challenges, and find fulfillment in completing tasks.

Rather than focusing solely on the finish line, enjoy the process of working toward your goals. Each step you complete is part of a more extensive journey, and by finding joy in the small moments, you can stay motivated and energized.

Celebrating minor achievements builds momentum and gives you a sense of progress and accomplishment. Every task, no matter how small, offers opportunities to learn and grow.

By embracing the journey, you can absorb the lessons of each experience. These lessons can contribute to personal and professional growth, making you more effective in future tasks.

Resilience In The Face Of Challenges

Challenges are inevitable, but how you respond to them is critical. Instead of becoming discouraged when things don't go as planned, adopt a mindset of adaptability.

View setbacks as opportunities to refine your approach, learn new skills, or discover better solutions. This flexibility helps you stay on course even when unexpected difficulties arise.

Obstacles are not barriers but stepping stones to success. Facing and overcoming challenges strengthens your resolve and builds your capacity for handling future difficulties.

By embracing the journey's ups and downs, you develop resilience and perseverance, essential for finishing strong.

The Power Of Support

A robust support system is crucial in helping you stay on track and finish what you start. Whether through accountability partners or mentors, surrounding yourself with people who encourage and guide you can significantly improve your ability to achieve your goals.

Having an accountability partner can provide motivation and support. Share your goals with someone you trust—whether a friend, family member or colleague—who can regularly check in on your progress.

This mutual accountability fosters a sense of responsibility, encouraging you to stay committed to your tasks.

Celebrating Accomplishments

Celebrating your accomplishments is a vital part of the finishing process. Acknowledging your hard work reinforces positive feelings and sets the stage for future success.

After completing a task, take a moment to reflect on the journey you took to get there. Consider the challenges you faced, the skills you developed, and the lessons you learned. This reflection helps you appreciate the hard work and dedication that went into your accomplishment.

Completing one task opens the door to new opportunities. After finishing, take time to evaluate what you want to pursue next. This evaluation can involve setting new goals that align with your passions and aspirations, keeping you engaged and motivated.

Setting new goals creates a continuous cycle of growth and achievement.

As you complete tasks and celebrate those accomplishments, you build momentum that propels you forward. This cycle enhances your fulfillment and encourages a proactive personal and professional development approach.

The Connection Between Consistency And Success

Success is often viewed as a destination, a final achievement that marks the end of a journey. However, many overlook that success is primarily built upon the foundation of consistency. Consistency is vital in achieving lasting results in personal growth, professional development, or spiritual journeys.

A building requires a solid foundation; achieving success demands a consistent approach. Consistency helps you establish a reliable routine that keeps you on track and focused on your objectives. Understanding the power of habit formation is essential for achieving our goals and making lasting changes in our lives.

Developing good habits can enhance our productivity, well-being, and overall success. Consistency is critical to forming lasting habits. Research suggests that it takes an average of 66 days for a new behavior to become automatic.

This means that if you consistently practice a new habit daily, it gradually becomes a natural part of your routine. The more you engage in a behavior, the more ingrained it becomes in your daily life.

It's essential to set realistic expectations when trying to establish new habits. Acknowledge that it may take time and effort, and don't be discouraged by setbacks. Instead, focus on small victories along the way.

Celebrate each day you successfully practice your new habit. This positive reinforcement will help you stay motivated. As you consistently engaging in a behavior evolves from a conscious effort to an unconscious pattern.

Initially, you may need to remind yourself to act, but it becomes a natural response over time. This shift reduces the mental effort required to continue the behavior, making it more sustainable in the long run.

You can leverage your existing habits to create new ones. For example, if you already have a morning routine that includes brushing your teeth, you can add a new habit, like stretching, right after that action.

This technique, known as "habit stacking," makes integrating new behaviors into your life easier as they build on established routines.

Success is often the result of small, consistent actions taken over time. For instance, reading just a few pages of a book daily may seem minor, but this daily commitment can accumulate vast knowledge and personal growth over months or years.

The key is recognizing that these small steps contribute to a more extensive journey, paving the way for substantial change. Rather than aiming for drastic changes, focus on maintaining manageable habits.

For example, to get fit, start with a ten-minute walk daily. Over time, you can gradually increase the duration and intensity of your workouts. This gradual approach prevents you from being overwhelmed and makes sticking with your new habits easier.

Consistency creates momentum, which is essential for staying motivated. When you consistently work toward your goals, you build confidence in your abilities and reinforce your commitment to your journey.

This growing confidence can help you overcome obstacles and overcome challenges that may arise. Developing a routine that incorporates your goals can help you maintain momentum.

When your desired actions become a regular part of your day, they require less mental energy, allowing you to focus on other aspects of your life.

For example, if you want to improve your writing skills, setting aside time each day to write—even if it's just a few sentences—will help solidify this habit and build momentum.

Consistency provides stability during challenging times. When you have established habits, they serve as anchors, helping you stay grounded when faced with setbacks or obstacles.

For instance, if your goal is to maintain a healthy lifestyle, regular exercise and meal planning habits can help you quickly return to your routine after experiencing a stressful period.

This anchoring effect allows you to bounce back more effectively. Regularly practicing consistency can help build mental toughness, which is crucial for overcoming adversity.

Each time you face a challenge and rely on your established habits to push through, you reinforce your ability to cope with difficulties. This repeated practice strengthens your resilience, making it easier to handle future setbacks.

Consistency fosters a mindset of learning and growth. When you regularly engage in a practice, you gain insights into what works and doesn't.

This ongoing process of reflection allows you to adapt your strategies and approaches based on your experiences. For example, if you're learning a new skill and encounter obstacles, your consistent practice helps you identify areas for improvement.

By maintaining consistency, you establish a continuous feedback loop. Regularly assessing your progress helps you recognize patterns in your behavior and outcomes, allowing you to refine your approach over time.

This process enhances your skills and builds your resilience as you learn to view mistakes as valuable opportunities for growth rather than failures.

The Power Of Consistency

Consistency requires you to stick to your commitments and build self-discipline. You reinforce your willpower each time you follow through on your plans—exercising regularly, studying for a set time, or working on a project.

Over time, this strengthens your ability to resist temptations and distractions, making staying committed to your goals easier. The self-discipline gained from consistent practices doesn't just apply to one area; it spills over into other aspects of your life.

For example, if you consistently manage your time well for studying, you might also become more disciplined in your work or personal life. This holistic improvement helps create a balanced and focused lifestyle.

When you engage in consistent action, your goals remain in your mind. This consistent engagement helps you develop a clear vision of what you want to achieve, making it less likely for you to lose sight of your objectives.

The more you repeat your efforts, the more ingrained your goals become in your daily routine. Consistency helps sharpen your focus by making you more aware of distractions that can lead you astray.

When you commit to a regular practice, you become adept at identifying what pulls you away from your goals. This awareness enables you to take proactive steps to minimize distractions and maintain your trajectory toward success.

Consistency In Relationships

Consistency fosters trust in any relationship. Communicating regularly and providing ongoing support helps others feel secure in the relationship.

For example, checking in on a friend consistently or being there for family members during tough times builds a sense of intimacy and understanding. This reliability creates a safe space for deeper connections to flourish.

When people know they can count on you consistently, it strengthens the bonds of friendship and partnership. Your actions and presence signal to others that you care about them, enhancing their emotional investment in the relationship.

This foundation of trust encourages open communication and strengthens the relationship over time. Consistency in your interactions encourages others to reciprocate your efforts.

When you regularly show up for others—whether through small gestures, quality time, or emotional support—you foster a culture of giving and receiving.

This reciprocal support creates a network where everyone feels empowered to reach out and assist each other. A supportive community thrives on consistency.

When everyone is committed to nurturing their relationships, it creates an environment where individuals feel safe to pursue their goals and dreams.

This collective effort enhances personal success and strengthens the community, leading to shared achievements and deeper connections.

Spiritual Growth

Regular practices such as prayer, meditation, and studying Scripture play a vital role in spiritual growth. When you commit to these activities consistently, you open the door to a closer relationship with God.

This ongoing engagement helps you understand His character, promises, and plans for your life. As you invest time in prayer and reflection, you cultivate a sense of purpose and direction.

This enables you to navigate life's challenges with faith and confidence. A consistent spiritual practice serves as a foundation during difficult times.

When faced with trials, your established relationship with God offers comfort and guidance. Scripture reminds us that God is always with us (*"So do not fear, for I am with you; do not be frightened, for I am your God. I will strengthen you and help you; I will uphold you with my righteous right hand."* Isaiah 41:10, NIV).

This reliance on God enhances your resilience and reinforces your trust in His sovereignty and goodness.

Consistency enables you to live out your values and beliefs authentically. When your actions align with your principles, you cultivate integrity.

This authenticity reflects your faith and allows you to be a positive example to others, demonstrating the transformative power of living according to God's Word.

Living consistently according to your beliefs leads to greater fulfillment and success in your spiritual journey.

When your daily choices reflect your values, you experience a sense of harmony and purpose. This alignment deepens your relationship with God and encourages you to impact others positively.

CHAPTER SIX

RECOGNIZING
AND SEIZING
OPPORTUNITIES

An opportunity is a favorable chance to do something or progress in life. It can take many forms, such as job openings, networking events, personal growth experiences, or unique situations that align with one's goals.

Opportunities often require a proactive approach. They may not present themselves clearly; instead, they might be disguised as challenges or changes. Learning to see beyond the surface is crucial in recognizing their potential.

To recognize opportunities, you need to be open and aware of your surroundings. Consider trends, conversations, and developments in your field and community. This awareness can help you spot potential opportunities before they become apparent.

Listening to others and observing the world can provide insights into emerging opportunities. Engaging with people, asking questions, and being curious can lead to valuable discoveries.

Sometimes, you may feel a sense of excitement or intuition about a particular situation. Trusting your instincts can help you recognize opportunities that resonate with your goals and values.

Understanding your goals and aspirations is essential for recognizing opportunities that align with them. Take time to reflect on what you want to achieve in different areas of life, such as career, relationships, and personal growth.

Visualizing your ideal future can help you identify opportunities that fit your aspirations. Consider what success looks like for you, and use this vision as a guide to evaluate potential opportunities.

Sometimes, opportunities come in unexpected forms. Being open to change and adaptable in your plans can help you embrace new possibilities you might otherwise overlook.

A growth mindset encourages continuous learning and improvement. When you approach life believing that you can develop your abilities and adapt to new situations, you're more likely to recognize and seize opportunities.

Instead of seeing obstacles as setbacks, view them as opportunities for growth. Challenges can lead to valuable lessons and experiences that prepare you for future opportunities.

Fear of failure can hold you back from seizing opportunities. Embrace the idea that failure is a natural part of the learning process. Every setback can provide valuable insights and pave the way for future successes.

Recognizing an opportunity is only the first step; you must also be ready to act. Ensure you have the necessary skills, knowledge, and resources to take advantage of the opportunities you identify.

When you spot an opportunity, break it into smaller, actionable steps. This approach makes the opportunity feel more manageable and helps you maintain momentum.

Seizing opportunities often requires stepping outside your comfort zone. Assess the risks involved, and be willing to take calculated risks to pursue your goals.

Remember that great rewards often come from taking bold

actions.

Networking is a powerful tool for recognizing and seizing opportunities. Building relationships with others can lead to valuable connections and insights that help you identify potential opportunities.

Talk about your aspirations with friends, family, and colleagues. By sharing your goals, you increase the chances that someone might point out an opportunity that aligns with what you want to achieve.

When you support others in their endeavors, you create a mutual assistance network. This culture of helping one another can lead to collaborative opportunities and new possibilities.

Take time to reflect on past opportunities you've encountered. What worked well? What didn't? Understanding your experiences can help you recognize patterns and improve your ability to spot future opportunities.

The Courage To Act On Divine Guidance

Divine guidance can manifest in many ways, including through Scripture, prayer, wise individuals' counsel, or the Holy Spirit's gentle promptings. Each avenue offers unique insights into God's will and intentions for our lives.

To truly hear God, we need to cultivate a habit of listening. This means setting aside time for prayer, reading Scripture, and being still in His presence.

Being attentive and open-hearted creates a space where God can speak to and guide us effectively.

Understanding and acting on divine guidance involves discerning what God wants us to do. This process requires prayerful reflection and seeking clarity about His desires for our lives.

Questions like *"What is God asking me to do?"* or *"How does this decision align with my faith?"* can help us navigate our choices.

We become more attuned to His leadership as we deepen our relationship with God through consistent prayer and study. This growth enables us to recognize His voice amidst the noise of daily life, helping us to make decisions that reflect His will.

Fear is a common barrier that can hinder us from acting on divine guidance. We may fear failure, rejection, or the unknown. The first step to overcoming fear is to acknowledge it. By recognizing our fears, we take control rather than allowing them to control us.

While fear is a natural human emotion, it shouldn't dictate our actions. The Bible encourages us to be strong and courageous (*"Have I not commanded you? Be strong and courageous. Do not be afraid; do not be discouraged, for the Lord your God will be with you wherever you go."* Joshua 1:9).

Remember, many biblical figures faced fears but trusted God, allowing Him to guide them through their challenges. It's common to doubt whether we can fulfill the tasks ahead of us. However, we can find the courage to step forward when we trust God's plan and ability to equip us.

In Jeremiah 29:11, the Bible reassures us that God has a good plan for our lives—*one that brings hope and a future.* Holding on to this promise can help dispel doubts, reminding us that God's guidance is rooted in love and purpose.

Courage doesn't always manifest in big, bold moves. Often, it's about embracing small actions of obedience. These small steps may seem insignificant, but they are essential in our walk with God.

Each act of faith, no matter how small, leads to more significant opportunities and experiences. For instance, saying a kind word to someone in need or praying for guidance can open doors to new possibilities.

Each step we take builds our confidence and strengthens our resolve. Looking back at our small actions, we see how God has worked through them, encouraging us to continue moving forward in faith. This process helps us realize that every small step contributes to the bigger picture of God's plan for our lives.

Once we sense God's direction, committing to action is vital. This commitment requires determination and a willingness to move forward, even when the path seems unclear.

He remembered that acting on divine guidance often means stepping into the unknown and trusting that God is leading us. God usually reveals more of His plan as we take steps in faith.

We might not see the entire journey before us, but by taking that first step, we trust He will guide us. As we act obediently, we open ourselves to new insights and opportunities God has prepared for us.

We must recognize that challenges may arise when we act on divine guidance.

These obstacles can take many forms—doubts, external pressures, or unforeseen circumstances. Expecting difficulties prepares us mentally and spiritually, allowing us to face them courageously.

Despite our challenges, we can find comfort in knowing God gives us the strength to overcome.

In times of difficulty, we can lean on His promises, reminding ourselves that we are not alone in our struggles.

Philippians 4:13 reminds us, *"I can do all things through Christ who strengthens me,"* assuring us that His power is made perfect in our weaknesses.

Failure is a natural part of life and often provides valuable lessons. When we stumble or fall short of our expectations, we must remember that failure doesn't define us.

Instead of allowing it to deter us, we can view it as a learning opportunity to reassess our approach, strengthen our resolve, and grow.

God's grace covers our shortcomings and failures. When we acknowledge our mistakes and seek His guidance, we open ourselves to His transformative power.

Each setback can lead to deeper understanding and greater resilience, reminding us that our journey of faith is not about perfection but about progress.

We often witness God's faithfulness when we act courageously on divine guidance. He may open doors we never imagined or provide the support we need

Embracing Courageous Faith

We often witness God's faithfulness when we act courageously on divine guidance. He may open doors we never imagined or provide the support we need at just the right moment.

These experiences reinforce our faith and encourage us to continue taking bold steps. Our willingness to act on divine guidance can ripple effect on those around us.

By stepping out in faith, we can inspire others to do the same, creating a chain of encouragement and courage within our communities.

Cultivating Courage

Developing a courageous mindset takes intentionality and practice. We can start by praying for boldness and asking God to help us overcome our fears and insecurities.

Seeking opportunities to step out in faith, even in small ways, can build our confidence. For example, volunteering for a new role in church or speaking up in a discussion can be steps toward living courageously.

Courage doesn't always mean making giant leaps; it can begin with small, consistent actions. Each time we face our fears, we reinforce our capacity for courage.

Over time, these small acts of faith can lead to more significant challenges that require even more trust in God. Regularly reminding ourselves of God's promises can bolster our courage and determination.

Recalling Scripture that speaks to God's faithfulness can provide comfort and encouragement when we face obstacles. For instance, *"Have I not commanded you? Be strong and courageous. Do not be afraid; do not be discouraged, for the Lord your God will be with you wherever you go."* (Joshua 1:9, NIV).

Keeping a journal of God's promises and past experiences where we've seen His faithfulness can be a powerful reminder.

When challenges arise, we can look back and see how God has led us before, reinforcing our trust in His goodness and plans for the future.

CHAPTER SEVEN

OVERCOMING
SPIRITUAL BARRIERS

Spiritual barriers separate us from God or disrupt our spiritual growth. They can manifest as negative thoughts, unhealthy behaviors, or external circumstances challenging our faith.

These barriers can lead to feelings of isolation, frustration, and confusion. They can create a disconnection from God, making it challenging to feel His presence or guidance in our lives.

When we allow barriers to persist, our spiritual growth can stagnate. We may find it challenging to engage in prayer, worship, or study of Scripture, hindering our ability to deepen our relationship with God.

Barriers can also make us more vulnerable to temptation. We may be more easily swayed by negative influences and worldly distractions when we are distant from God.

Overcoming spiritual barriers is not about perfection but about grace. God's grace is sufficient for our weaknesses, as stated in *"...My grace is sufficient for you, for my power is made perfect in weakness."* (2 Corinthians 12:9, NIV).

Embracing the truth that He loves us unconditionally and desires to help us overcome our struggles is crucial.

Recognize that spiritual growth is a journey. Be patient with yourself as you work through barriers. God is faithful to guide you every step of the way.

As you overcome spiritual barriers, you will experience greater freedom in your relationship with God. This freedom allows you to serve Him wholeheartedly and live out your faith authentically.

Identifying Obstacles To Spiritual Growth

Spiritual growth is deepening our relationship with God and becoming more like Christ in thought, behavior, and character.

It involves maturing in our faith, growing our understanding of God's Word, and living in alignment with His will.

Spiritual growth encompasses every aspect of our Christian life—how we read and apply Scripture, pray and seek God's presence, and express our faith in our actions and interactions with others.

Just as a plant needs essential elements like sunlight, water, and nutrients to grow, spiritual growth requires nourishment.

We need to feed our faith with the Word of God, pray, fellowship with other believers, and obey His commands.

Spiritual growth strengthens our ability to face difficulties with faith and resilience.

As we grow in our understanding of God's promises and trust in His plan, we are better equipped to navigate life's challenges.

Spiritual growth transforms us from the inside out, helping us to reflect Christ's love, patience, humility, and compassion.

Over time, we develop traits that align more closely with Jesus' character, becoming living testimonies of His grace. As we grow spiritually, we become more attuned to God's purpose for our lives.

Spiritual growth helps us discern His guidance and empowers us to live out His unique calling and fulfill His plans.

Common Obstacles To Spiritual Growth

Busyness and Distraction

In our busy, technology-driven era, busyness and distractions can quickly take over our lives, pulling our attention away from what truly matters—our relationship with God.

With constant responsibilities, tasks, and technology demanding our time, we may be overwhelmed and neglect essential spiritual practices.

When our schedules are full, we often neglect our time with God—prayer, worship, and Bible study.

Yet, these spiritual disciplines are vital for our growth, peace, and strength.

Without them, we can feel disconnected from God, spiritually drained, and less equipped to handle life's challenges.

To overcome the effects of busyness and distraction, we must prioritize our spiritual life, setting aside intentional time for God amidst our daily responsibilities.

This helps us focus on what matters most—nurturing our relationship with Him.

Doubt and Unbelief

Doubt and unbelief can act as significant barriers to spiritual growth.

Doubts about God's existence, goodness, or promises can distance us from Him.

These uncertainties make it harder to trust in His plan, engage with His Word, or seek Him in prayer.

In moments of doubt, it's essential to remember that questioning is a natural part of faith.

Even firm believers in the Bible, like Thomas and David, had moments of doubt.

The key is to bring those doubts to God and seek understanding through prayer, Scripture, and counsel from others.

Confronting our doubts with faith opens the door to more profound growth, allowing God to strengthen our belief and renew our trust in Him.

Sin and Guilt

Sin and guilt can become significant obstacles to spiritual growth.

When we fall into sin, it often leads to feelings of guilt and shame, which can create a sense of separation from God.

This distance makes it difficult to approach Him in prayer or engage in spiritual practices, as we may feel unworthy or fear rejection.

However, it's essential to remember that God's grace is more significant than our sin.

"If we confess our sins, he is faithful and just and will forgive us our sins and purify us from all unrighteousness." (1 John 1:9, NIV)

Acknowledging our mistakes, repenting, and seeking His forgiveness allows us to overcome guilt and restore our relationship with Him, creating a pathway for renewed spiritual growth.

Fear of Change

Fear of change can be a significant barrier to spiritual growth. Growth often means stepping out of familiar routines or comfort zones, which can be unsettling.

We might resist taking on new challenges, confronting brutal truths, or deepening our faith because of the uncertainty that change brings.

However, embracing change is essential for growth.

"Do not conform to the pattern of this world, but be transformed by the renewing of your mind." (Romans 12:2, NIV)

This continual transformation requires us to trust in God's guidance, knowing He leads us through change for our benefit and spiritual maturity.

Surrounding ourselves with people or environments that do not support our faith can impact our spiritual growth.

Negative influences can lead us away from God and His truth.

Identifying Your Obstacles

Self-Reflection

Self-reflection is a valuable tool for identifying barriers to spiritual growth. By evaluating your spiritual journey honestly, you can pinpoint the areas where you may struggle.

Whether it's busyness, doubt, fear, or something else, self-awareness is the first step toward overcoming these obstacles.

Journaling your thoughts is a practical way to reflect. It helps clarify your feelings and experiences, allowing you to see patterns holding you back.

As you write, pray for insight and ask God to reveal the areas where you need growth, just as *"Search me, God, and know my heart; test me and know my anxious thoughts. See if there is any offensive way in me and lead me in the way everlasting."* (Psalm 139:23-24, NIV).

Evaluate Your Time

Evaluating your time is essential for identifying distractions that may take priority over your spiritual growth.

Take a close look at how you spend your day.

Are there activities, like excessive screen time or over-commitments, that consume your time and energy?

By recognizing these time drains, you can adjust to create more space for prayer, Bible study, and reflection.

As Ephesians 5:15-16 encourages us, *"Be very careful, then, how you live—not as unwise but as wise, making the most of every opportunity."* (NIV)

Assess Your Mindset

Assessing your mindset is crucial for identifying beliefs or attitudes hindering your spiritual growth.

Reflect on your thoughts and feelings about God—are there doubts, fears, or misconceptions that prevent you from fully trusting Him?

Understanding your mindset can help uncover obstacles like unbelief or fear of change.

As Romans 12:2 reminds us, *"Do not conform to the pattern of this world but be transformed by the renewing of your mind."* (NIV)

Seek Feedback

Seek feedback from trusted friends, mentors, or leaders about your spiritual journey.

Sometimes, others can offer a perspective you might not see alone.

They may notice patterns, challenges, or strengths that you overlook.

By sharing your experiences and listening to their insights, you can gain valuable guidance on areas where you may need growth or identify hidden obstacles.

Proverbs 11:14 reminds us, *"In the multitude of counselors, there is safety."* (NIV)

Trusted counsel can help you move forward with wisdom and encouragement.

The Role Of Faith In Overcoming Obstacles

Trust in God's power to help you overcome any barriers to spiritual growth.

Remember, you are not relying on your strength but on His.

"I can do all things through Christ who strengthens me." (Philippians 4:13, NIV)

When challenges arise, whether doubt, fear, or distractions, God's power is more significant than any obstacle.

Lean on Him in times of weakness, and He will give you the strength to persevere and grow in your faith.

Focusing on God's promises in Scripture is a powerful way to encourage and uplift one's spirit during one's journey of spiritual growth.

Meditating on these truths reminds us of God's faithfulness and love.

Promises like *"For I know the plans I have for you"* (Jeremiah 29:11, NIV) can reassure you that God has a purpose for your life.

These promises are a foundation of hope, providing strength when facing challenges.

Embrace them as you work through obstacles, allowing them to guide you toward deeper faith and understanding.

Embracing growth opportunities involves being open to new experiences that challenge and expand your faith.

Consider participating in activities that push you beyond your comfort zone.

Volunteering for various ministries helps others and deepens your spiritual journey.

You can learn to apply your faith practically, build relationships, and gain valuable insights from fellow believers.

Joining a Bible study group offers a supportive environment to explore Scripture and discuss its application.

It encourages accountability and fosters deeper understanding through shared insights.

Serving those in need allows you to live out your faith actively.

Engaging with different communities can broaden your perspective, inspire empathy, and help you develop new skills.

Embracing these opportunities enables you to grow spiritually and strengthens your trust in God as you navigate the challenges of stepping out of faith.

Each experience contributes to your personal growth and deepens your relationship with God.

The Power Of Distress As A Spiritual Alarm

Distress is an emotional state characterized by significant suffering or pain.

It can arise from various situations, including loss, disappointment, conflict, and fear.

Distress often forces us to confront uncomfortable emotions and situations, prompting us to seek resolution and healing.

It can manifest in various ways, including sadness, anger, anxiety, or physical symptoms like headaches or fatigue.

Recognizing distress is the first step toward addressing the underlying issues and finding ways to cope and heal.

The Role Of Distress In Our Lives

While distress is often viewed negatively, it can also serve as a powerful tool for growth.

Just as a fire can refine gold, distress can refine our character and deepen our faith.

Recognizing Distress as a Spiritual Alarm

Distress often acts as a wake-up call, illuminating aspects of our lives that may require urgent attention.

When we experience distress, it often highlights recurring behaviors or habits that may be detrimental to our well-being.

For example, feelings of constant anxiety might indicate that we are not prioritizing self-care or trusting God's plan.

Recognizing these patterns allows us to take steps toward change.

Distress can illuminate relationships that drain us emotionally or spiritually. It can prompt us to evaluate whether certain connections align with our values and whether they are fostering growth or harm.

Distress invites us to pause and reflect on our lives. It urges us to ask critical questions: *Am I living in alignment with my values? Am I nurturing my spiritual well-being?*

This self-reflection can lead to important insights and decisions. Just as a physical alarm alerts us to danger, distress can signal that something needs to change.

This awareness can motivate us to seek healing through prayer, counseling, or other means.

It encourages us to confront issues head-on rather than ignore them.

Distress can lead us to explore our faith more deeply. For guidance and comfort, we may turn to Scripture, prayer, and community support during challenging times. This pursuit can strengthen our spiritual understanding and connection with God.

When we experience distress, it often forces us to pause and reflect on our circumstances.

This reflection can lead to greater self-awareness and a desire to seek God's guidance in our struggles.

In Psalm 46:1, we are reminded that *"God is our refuge and strength, an ever-present help in trouble."* (NIV)

The Call to Seek God in Distress

Distress often acts as a catalyst, drawing us nearer to God and encouraging us to seek His presence. When faced with distress, we become acutely aware of our limitations and vulnerabilities. This realization can lead us to acknowledge our need for God's strength, wisdom, and guidance, prompting us to turn to Him in our time of need.

Distress can prompt heartfelt prayers as we pour our emotions and struggles before God. This act of reaching out helps us to articulate our fears, anxieties, and desires, creating an open channel for communication with our Creator.

In moments of distress, we often seek solace in God's promises and presence. Turning to Scripture can provide comfort and encouragement, reminding us of God's faithfulness and love.

"Cast all your anxiety on him because he cares for you." (1 Peter 5:7, NIV) encourages us to release our burdens to Him, offering reassurance that we are not alone in our struggles.

Distress can lead us to seek God's guidance more earnestly. Prayer, meditation, and Bible reading can help us gain insights and direction for our circumstances.

God may clarify the next steps we need to take or reveal more profound truths about ourselves and our situations. Turning to God in distress can ultimately strengthen our faith.

As we experience His presence and see how He helps us navigate our challenges, we grow in our trust in Him. This trust can empower us to face future difficulties confidently, knowing that God is always with us.

David, for instance, often poured out his heart to God in the Psalms, expressing his fears and frustrations.

Distress as a Catalyst for Change

While uncomfortable, distress can serve as a powerful catalyst for change. Emotional distress often indicates that something in our lives needs attention. Whether it's a toxic relationship, unhealthy habit, or lack of spiritual nourishment, distress brings these issues to the forefront, forcing us to address them.

This can lead to re-evaluating our current lifestyle, priorities, and behaviors.

Distress often shakes us out of complacency. When we feel discomfort or pain, we are more likely to recognize areas where we've been stagnant or resistant to change.

This recognition can propel us to take action we've been avoiding, such as mending broken relationships, confronting personal shortcomings, or pursuing growth opportunities that previously felt intimidating.

When distress motivates us to act, it often leads to decisions aimed at long-term well-being and spiritual growth.

Whether we adjust our daily routines to incorporate more prayer and reflection, seek professional or spiritual counseling, or address unresolved conflicts, distress can push us toward actions that promote healing and growth.

Distress from unresolved guilt, shame, or broken relationships can motivate us to seek forgiveness and restore peace. This can involve apologizing to others, making amends, or offering forgiveness ourselves. Doing so opens doors for healing and more profound spiritual growth.

Ultimately, distress can motivate us to realign our lives with God's will. Whether through repentance, seeking guidance, or committing to new spiritual disciplines, distress can become the turning point that leads us back to a closer relationship with God.

Navigating through distress can teach us valuable lessons about ourselves, our faith, and our relationship with God. These lessons often lead to a deeper understanding of God's grace and a stronger faith foundation.

Transforming Distress into Spiritual Growth

Prayer is essential in transforming distress into spiritual growth. When we pray, we invite God into our struggles, allowing Him to work in our hearts and minds.

In Philippians 4:6-7, we are encouraged to bring our anxieties to God, who promises to provide *"peace that surpasses understanding."*(NIV)

Experiencing and overcoming distress can build spiritual resilience. Each challenge faced and overcome through faith strengthens our character and deepens our trust in God.

Distress is a common human experience that everyone encounters at different points in their lives. Acknowledging that we are not alone in our struggles can provide comfort and help us approach distress with a sense of solidarity.

Realizing that even strong figures in faith, like David or Job, faced distress can remind us that it's a normal part of the human journey.

Instead of viewing distress solely as a negative experience, we can learn to see it as an opportunity for growth and transformation.

We can approach distress with curiosity rather than fear by shifting our perspective. This mindset allows us to explore what we can learn from our experiences and how to grow through them.

Accepting distress as part of life can help us develop resilience. When we embrace challenges, we strengthen our ability to cope with future difficulties.

Over time, we learn that while distress is uncomfortable, it is temporary and can lead to valuable insights and growth.

Distress can draw us closer to God, reminding us of our need for His presence and support. When we accept distress as part of life, we can turn to Him for comfort and guidance. This dependence can deepen our faith and enhance our spiritual growth.

Accepting our distress can lead to greater empathy for the struggles of others. When we recognize that everyone faces challenges, we can be more compassionate and supportive, fostering community and connection.

Regularly reflecting on our distressing experiences can help us identify patterns and areas for growth. Journaling or discussing our feelings with a trusted friend can aid in processing our experiences and finding clarity.

CHAPTER EIGHT

THE PRINCIPLES
OF ABUNDANCE

Abundance is the state of having more than enough. It signifies prosperity, fullness, and overflow in all aspects of life. It goes beyond mere material possessions and includes emotional and spiritual richness.

An abundance mindset believes that there are enough resources, opportunities, and blessings for everyone. This contrasts with a scarcity mindset, which views resources as limited and often leads to fear and competition.

As Jesus promises, *"I have come that they may have life and have it abundantly."* (John 10:10, NIV), reflecting God's intention for us to live fully and richly.

Gratitude And Abundance

Gratitude is a crucial principle of abundance. When we express thankfulness for what we have, we open ourselves to receiving even more.

"Give thanks in all circumstances." (1 Thessalonians 5:18, NIV) encourages us to recognize the abundance already in our lives.

Overcoming Scarcity

Recognizing and overcoming a scarcity mentality is essential to embracing abundance. This mentality may manifest as fear of lack, jealousy of others, or a reluctance to share.

Self-awareness is the first step to change. Practicing positive affirmations and surrounding ourselves with encouraging people can help cultivate an abundance mindset.

By focusing on opportunities instead of limitations, we can shift our perspective toward a more abundant outlook.

Nurturing Abundance

Our environment influences our mindset. Surrounding ourselves with people with an abundance mindset can encourage us to adopt similar beliefs.

Engaging in communities that promote positivity and support helps nurture a sense of abundance. Establishing a physical and emotional space that fosters growth is vital. This may include decluttering our surroundings, creating peaceful spaces for reflection, and engaging in activities that inspire creativity and joy.

Setting clear intentions for what we want to achieve helps us align our actions with our desires. By focusing on our goals and visualizing success, we cultivate an abundance mindset that attracts opportunities.

Trusting In The Miraculous

An abundance mindset believes in the miraculous. By trusting that God can provide beyond our expectations, we open ourselves to experience His blessings in unexpected ways.

Understanding God's Provision

Provision refers to the act of supplying what is necessary for life. In the context of faith, it means recognizing that God meets our physical and spiritual needs.

As Philippians 4:19 reminds us, *"And my God will supply every need of yours according to his riches in glory in Christ Jesus."* (NIV)

While God indeed cares for our physical needs—such as food, shelter, and safety—His provision also extends to our emotional and spiritual needs. He offers peace in times of trouble, strength in weakness, and wisdom when we seek guidance.

God's Miraculous Provision

The Israelites, after being liberated from slavery in Egypt, encountered numerous challenges, including hunger and thirst.

Instead of abandoning them, God showed His care by miraculously providing for their needs. God provided the Israelites with manna, an exceptional bread-like food, daily.

This daily provision taught them reliance on Him. In Exodus 16:4, God instructed them to gather only what they needed each day, emphasizing the importance of trusting Him daily. This reflects God's desire that we depend on Him for our needs rather than try to rely solely on our strength.

In Exodus 17:6, when the Israelites were thirsty, God instructed Moses to strike a rock from which water miraculously flowed. This act quenched their physical thirst and reminded them of God's ability to give life from unexpected sources.

Provision in Desperate Times

In 1 Kings 17, Israel faced a severe drought, leading to famine and suffering. God sent the prophet Elijah to a widow in Zarephath, outside Israel, who was gathering sticks to prepare a last meal for herself and her son.

This situation illustrates the depth of her need and the hopelessness she felt. When Elijah asked the widow for water and a piece of bread, she expressed her despair, revealing that she had only a handful of flour and a little oil left.

Despite her dire circumstances, Elijah assured her that if she made him a small loaf first, her flour and oil would not run out until the drought ended (1 Kings 17:13-14). This required a significant act of faith, which meant sharing what little she had.

The widow obeyed Elijah's instructions, and God miraculously multiplied her resources. The flour and oil did not run out during the drought, demonstrating God's ability to provide abundantly even when circumstances seem impossible (1 Kings 17:15-16).

The Power of Faith

This provision showcases how God can turn our limited resources into something sufficient for our needs. The widow's willingness to trust Elijah's word reflects the power of faith.

She acted in faith, believing that God would provide, and her obedience resulted in miraculous provision. This story encourages us to trust God, even when our situation seems desperate, and reminds us that He can work wonders with what we have.

The widow, a single mother in a famine, represents those in desperate situations.

God's intervention demonstrates His desire to care for those struggling, reminding us to look out for those in need.

The Heart of Faith

Faith is the heart of trusting in God's provision. It means believing that God knows our needs and cares deeply for us. This trust is not based on our circumstances but on God's character and promises.

When we cultivate faith, we learn to rely on Him, knowing He has a plan for our lives.

As Jesus reminds us in *"Do not worry about your life, what you will eat or drink; or about your body, what you will wear."* (Matthew 6:31-33, NIV)

Instead, He encourages us to *"seek first his kingdom and his righteousness."* (Matthew 6:33, NIV)

This means prioritizing our relationship with God and living according to His ways. We can trust that He will provide for our needs when we do this.

Faith in Action

Faith is essential in recognizing God's provision.

When we trust Him, we are more likely to see how He works in our lives, even in challenging circumstances.

This awareness can increase our gratitude and strengthen our faith, allowing us to navigate difficulties confidently.

Trusting God's provision also requires action.

It involves stepping out in faith, much like the widow did when she shared her last meal with Elijah.

Our faith can lead us to take necessary actions, such as generosity, helping others, or pursuing opportunities, knowing God will care for our needs.

Growing in Faith

Our faith can grow through experiences, prayer, and Scripture reading. As we witness God's provision in our lives, our faith deepens, enabling us to trust Him more fully in future challenges.

Faith in God's provision brings peace to our hearts. When we surrender our worries to Him and trust His goodness, we can experience calmness amid chaos. This peace comes from knowing that we are not alone and God is actively involved.

Trusting in God's provision also means letting go of anxiety about the future. When we worry, we often forget God's past faithfulness. Reflecting on how God has provided for us in the past can help strengthen our faith in His ability to do so in the present and future.

Recognizing God's Provision

Recognizing God's provision involves gratitude.

When we express thanks for what we have, we acknowledge God as the source of our blessings.

"Give thanks in all circumstances." (1 Thessalonians 5:18, NIV) reminds us to recognize every good gift comes from God.

A grateful heart opens our eyes to the abundance around us. When we focus on our blessings, we cultivate a mindset that sees God's provision everywhere. This perspective shifts our focus from lack to abundance, helping us live more joyfully.

Responsible Stewardship

Understanding God's provision also means being responsible stewards of what He provides. This includes managing our resources wisely, sharing with others, and not taking our blessings for granted.

"The wise store up choice food and olive oil." (Proverbs 21:20, NIV) teaches us to save for the future.

We are compelled to share with others when we recognize how richly God has provided for us. Acts of kindness and generosity reflect God's love and create a provisioning cycle in our communities.

"Give, and it will be given to you." (Luke 6:38, NIV) encourages us to give, reminding us that generosity leads to more blessings.

Overcoming Doubts

Doubts about God's provision can creep in, especially during tough times. In these moments, we must counter our doubts with God's promises.

Scriptures like *"Ask, and it will be given to you; seek and you will find."* (Matthew 7:7, NIV) remind us that if we ask, we will receive; if we seek, we will find.

Turning to God in prayer can help us overcome doubts. We cultivate a deeper trust in His provision by sharing our fears and needs with Him. Prayer helps us seek guidance and reassures us of God's presence and care.

Testimonies Of Faith

Many believers can recount times when God unexpectedly provided for their needs. These stories serve as powerful testimonies of God's faithfulness and can inspire others to trust in His provision.

Daniel 6's account of Daniel in the lion's den is a potent illustration of trust. Daniel believed in God's protection and provision even though he was sent into a lion's den for not giving up his faith. Daniel miraculously escaped unscathed when God sent an angel to close the lions' mouths, proving both God's faithfulness and Daniel's unwavering faith in Him.

Daniel 3's account of Shadrach, Meshach, and Abednego in the blazing furnace exemplifies their unshakable faith. They were cast into a raging fire for refusing to worship idols, yet God's presence miraculously kept them alive instead of causing them to perish.

They showed that they trusted God to save them by walking safely through the flames, and their faith was rewarded with supernatural intervention.

The Role Of Generosity In Blessing

Generosity is the willingness to give more than what is expected or required. It is an attitude of the heart that seeks to bless others without expecting anything in return.

Generosity can manifest in various forms, such as financial giving, volunteering time, offering encouragement, or simply being present for someone in need.

A generous heart reflects the character of God, who is the ultimate giver.

As John 3:16 reminds us, *"For God so loved the world that he gave his one and only Son."* (NIV)

When we adopt a generous spirit, we mirror God's love and kindness to the world.

The Spirit of Generosity

In Mark 12:41-44, Jesus observed a poor widow who put two small coins into the offering box. He praised her for giving all she had, demonstrating that true generosity is not measured by the amount shown but by the spirit behind the gift.

"For they all contributed out of their abundance, but she out of her poverty put in everything she had." (Mark 12:44, NIV)

This story illustrates that even small acts of generosity can significantly impact.

Generosity in Action

The parable of the Good Samaritan (Luke 10:25-37) showcases generosity in action.

Despite societal differences, the Samaritan helped a wounded traveler by caring for his injuries and meeting his needs.

This story teaches us that generosity transcends boundaries and can change lives.

The Power of Generosity

When we practice generosity, we become a channel of blessings for those in need. Acts of kindness can uplift others, provide comfort, and restore hope.

"You will be enriched in every way to be generous on every occasion." (2 Corinthians 9:11, NIV)

Our generosity can lead others to express gratitude and draw closer to God.

Generosity also enriches our own lives. When we give to others, we often experience a sense of fulfillment and joy.

"A generous person will prosper; whoever refreshes others will be refreshed." (Proverbs 11:25, NIV)

Cultivating Generosity

Generosity is contagious. Cultivating a culture of generosity within our families, churches, and communities inspires others to give. Creating opportunities for collective giving and serving fosters an environment where generosity flourishes.

Teaching children the value of generosity from a young age is essential.

Deuteronomy 6:7 encourages us to *"teach them to your children, talking about them when you sit at home and when you walk along the road, when you lie down and when you get up."* (NIV)

Overcoming Barriers to Generosity

Many people struggle with generosity due to fear of scarcity or insecurity about their resources. However, Philippians 4:19

reassures us that *"my God will meet all your needs according to the riches of his glory in Christ Jesus."* (NIV)

Trusting in God's provision can help alleviate fears about giving. Sometimes, people view generosity as a burden or obligation.

However, shifting our perspective to see the joy in giving can transform our attitude.

"Each of you should give what you have decided in your heart to give, not reluctantly or under compulsion, for God loves a cheerful giver." (2 Corinthians 9:7, NIV)

The Impact of Generosity

Generosity can lead to significant change in individuals and communities. When people come together to support one another, it fosters a sense of belonging and unity. This collective effort can address pressing social issues, relieve crises, and create a culture of support and care.

Generosity allows us to reflect God's love and compassion to the world.

"Let your light shine before others, that they may see your good deeds and glorify your Father in heaven." (Matthew 5:16, NIV)

Our generosity can lead others to encounter God's love and grace.

CHAPTER NINE

EMBRACING INSTRUCTIONS FOR LIFE

God desires to lead us through every season of life. As Proverbs 3:5-6 reminds us, "Trust in the Lord with all your heart and lean not on your understanding; in all your ways submit to him, and he will make your paths straight." (NIV)

When we seek God's wisdom, we allow Him to direct our paths and provide clarity in uncertain situations. Embracing divine instructions means recognizing that God's ways are higher than ours.

Isaiah 55:8-9 encourages us to acknowledge, *"For my thoughts are not your thoughts, neither are your ways my ways,"* and *"As the heavens are higher than the earth, so are my ways higher than your ways and my thoughts than your thoughts."* (NIV)

Scriptural Guidance

The Scriptures serve as a rich source of guidance and wisdom. Psalm 119:105 reminds us that *"Your word is a lamp for my feet, a light on my path."* (NIV)

Regularly reading and meditating on the Bible equips us with the knowledge to make wise choices.

However, it's not enough to merely read the Bible; we must apply its teachings.

James 1:22 urges us, *"Do not merely listen to the word, and so deceive yourselves. Do what it says."* (NIV)

Obedience and Transformation

Embracing instructions for life requires obedience, which can be challenging at times. We may encounter doubts, fears, or temptations to follow our desires.

However, Romans 12:2 reminds us, *"Do not conform to the pattern of this world, but be transformed by the renewing of your mind."* (NIV)

Choosing to follow God's instructions leads to blessings and fulfillment. Deuteronomy 28:1-2 speaks of the blessings that come from obeying God's commands.

When we align our lives with His guidance, we experience peace, purpose, and direction.

Intentional Living

Incorporating God's instructions into our daily lives requires intentionality.

Establishing daily prayer, Bible reading, and reflection can strengthen our understanding and application of His teachings.

A Life of Influence

As we embrace and live out God's instructions, we become a light to those around us.

Matthew 5:16 encourages us, *"Let your light shine before others, that they may see your good deeds and glorify your Father in heaven."* (NIV)

Our lives can inspire and influence others to seek His wisdom as well.

Seeking God's Will in Daily Decisions

Jeremiah 29:11 explains that God has a purpose and plan for us. His plans are not meant to harm us but to give us a future filled with hope.

Understanding this divine intention helps us realize that God desires the best for us and encourages us to seek His guidance in all our lives.

God's desire to guide us stems from His deep love for us. He wants to have a personal relationship with each of His children. This relationship allows us to experience His guidance through prayer, Bible reading, and the Holy Spirit's prompting.

When we engage with God personally, we can trust He will lead us in the right direction. Knowing that God is invested in our lives gives us the confidence to make decisions.

Instead of relying solely on our understanding or wisdom, we can lean on His guidance.

As Proverbs 3:5-6 reminds us, *"Trust in the Lord with all your heart and lean not on your understanding; in all your ways submit to him, and he will make your paths straight."* (NIV)

Prayer is vital to understanding God's desire for us. We invite His wisdom into our lives by bringing our concerns, questions, and decisions to Him.

As we pray, we cultivate a listening heart, allowing us to discern His voice and leading. When we immerse ourselves in Scripture, we gain insight into God's will and learn how to align our lives with His purposes.

God often guides us subtly, prompting us to take certain actions or make specific choices. Being open to His direction means stepping out in faith, even when the path ahead is uncertain. This willingness to follow His lead shows our trust in His plans.

When we acknowledge God's desire to guide us, we can experience peace amidst life's uncertainties. Instead of feeling overwhelmed or anxious about the future, we can rest assured that He is with us and has our best interests at heart.

We must acknowledge our need for God's wisdom in our decision-making.

By humbling ourselves and admitting our limitations, we open ourselves to receive His guidance. Before making any decision, take time to pray.

Approach Him with an open heart, seeking clarity and understanding about the choices before you.

James 1:5 assures us that if we lack wisdom, *"If any of you lacks wisdom, you should ask God, who gives generously to all without finding fault."* (NIV)

Ask God for wisdom in specific situations, and trust He will provide insight and direction. God speaks to us through His Word.

Spending time in Scripture allows us to gain insight into His character and His will for our lives. As we read the Bible, we identify principles that apply to our daily decisions.

For example, understanding the importance of honesty, integrity, and love can shape our choices in relationships, work, and other areas of life.

The Holy Spirit is our helper and guide.

John 14:26 reminds us that *"The Counselor, the Holy Spirit, whom the Father will send in my name, will teach you all things and remind you of everything I have commanded you."* (NIV)

Being attuned to the Holy Spirit's voice is essential for discerning God's will in our decisions. Pay attention to the inner promptings and convictions that the Holy Spirit may bring.

Sometimes, these may manifest as a sense of peace, discomfort, or clarity about a particular choice. Recognizing these promptings can guide us in making decisions that reflect God's will.

We must evaluate our current circumstances and opportunities as we seek God's will. Sometimes, God opens doors for us to walk through, leading us in specific directions. Observing these opportunities can help clarify His guidance.

Understanding God's timing is crucial. We must wait for God to reveal His will and trust He will guide us when the time is right. As we make decisions, we should consider God's character—His love, mercy, justice, and faithfulness.

Our decisions can significantly affect those around us. After seeking God's will and deciding, trust Him with the outcome.

Romans 8:28 assures us that *"And we know that in all things God works for the good of those who love him."* (NIV)

Even if the outcome is not what we expect, we can trust that God works for our good and His glory. Sometimes, seeking God's will requires taking steps of faith into the unknown. Embrace the journey, trusting that God will guide you as you take steps forward.

CHAPTER TEN

THE IMPACT OF SACRIFICE

Sacrifice means giving something up—be it time, resources, or comfort—for the benefit of others or in obedience to God. It requires a heart willing to let go of what is important to us for something more significant.

From Abraham's willingness to offer Isaac (Genesis 22) to Jesus laying down His life for humanity (John 15:13), these acts demonstrate the significant impact that sacrifice can have, leading to blessings, transformation, and divine favor. When we sacrifice for God, we deepen our relationship with Him.

Sacrifice requires faith and trust, which draw us closer to His heart. As James 4:8 reminds us, *"Draw near to God, and He will draw near to you."* (NIV)

Our willingness to let go of worldly attachments opens us to a more intimate walk with God. Sacrifice shapes our character, teaching us patience, humility, and perseverance.

We demonstrate love and commitment when we put others' needs before our own. This is particularly evident in family dynamics, where parents often sacrifice their time and desires for their children's well-being. Such actions build trust and deepen connections. When we model sacrificial living, we encourage others to do the same.

Sacrificial acts are pleasing to God. Our sacrifices reflect our devotion and commitment to Him. When we sacrifice, we often experience God's provision in unexpected ways.

Trusting Him with our sacrifices opens the door for His abundant blessings. Each of us is called to embrace sacrifice in different ways. It may involve serving in our communities, mentoring others, or giving generously to those in need.

Understanding our unique calling helps us fulfill God's purpose for our lives. We must be willing to take action to make an impact through sacrifice. This could mean volunteering, sharing resources, or being present for someone in need.

Taking steps towards sacrificial living requires courage but ultimately leads to fulfillment and joy.

Sacrifice transforms our perspective on life. It shifts our focus from self-centeredness to a greater awareness of others' needs. As we give, we find joy in serving rather than seeking personal gain.

When we touch one person's life, it often leads to them touching others, spreading love and kindness. This chain reaction demonstrates how sacrifice can bring about widespread change.

Understanding The Cost Of Discipleship

Discipleship involves more than just believing in Jesus; it means actively following Him and living according to His teachings. It is a lifelong commitment to grow in faith, share His message, and embody His love daily.

Self-denial is a crucial aspect of discipleship. In Luke 9:23, Jesus calls us to *"Take up your cross daily and follow me."* (NIV)

This surrender is not just a one-time act but a daily commitment to prioritize God's will over our own.

Self-denial requires us to release our plans, ambitions, and even dreams if they conflict with God's purpose for our lives. It may involve giving up things we hold dear, but in doing so, we gain something far more significant—intimacy with God and alignment with His perfect plan.

Following Jesus often requires stepping outside of our comfort zones.

Self-denial challenges us to embrace discomfort for the sake of spiritual growth. Whether giving up certain habits, resisting temptation, or accepting complex tasks, this sacrifice brings us closer to Christ's heart.

Jesus emphasizes that taking up our cross is a daily decision. Each day, we face choices reflecting our commitment to Christ— whether to live for ourselves or Him. This process of daily self-denial strengthens our character and draws us nearer to the Lord.

Self-denial is ultimately about trust. We must trust that God's plans are better than our own, even when we don't fully understand them. This surrender requires faith that God will guide us, provide for us, and fulfill His promises as we follow Him faithfully.

Jesus makes it clear in John 15:20 that His followers will face opposition: *"If they persecuted me, they will also persecute you."* (NIV)

Being a disciple of Christ means accepting that not everyone will understand or support our faith. We may encounter criticism, rejection, and even hostility because of our commitment to living according to God's Word.

Discipleship often involves standing firm in our beliefs, even when others disagree or challenge us. This can be especially difficult when opposition comes from people close to us, such as friends, family, or coworkers.

However, it is an opportunity to demonstrate Christ's love, grace, and truth in the face of adversity. When facing opposition, it's essential to respond Christ-like, showing patience and kindness, even when others are hostile.

Romans 12:14 reminds us, *"Bless those who persecute you; bless and do not curse them."* (NIV)

Our response to opposition can be a powerful testimony of our faith and reliance on God. Although opposition can feel discouraging, it is in these moments that we are called to lean on God's strength.

Trusting in God's presence and power enables us to persevere through difficult times. Facing opposition is part of the cost of discipleship.

Jesus warns that following Him may involve hardship and sacrifice (Matthew 16:24-25). However, we are also reminded that the reward of faithfully following Him is far greater than any earthly challenges we may face.

Our suffering is temporary, but the eternal life we gain through Christ is everlasting.

In Matthew 22:37, Jesus tells us the greatest commandment: *"Love the Lord your God with all your heart and with all your soul and with all your mind."* (NIV)

This is the foundation of true discipleship. It means giving God our full attention, affection, and devotion. Loving God wholeheartedly goes beyond feelings—it's reflected in how we live our lives and prioritize Him in our decisions.

Wholehearted devotion means making God the center of everything we do. We are called to put God first, whether it's our work, relationships, or daily routines. This might mean sacrificing personal desires or ambitions to align our lives with His will.

Our love for God should be evident in our actions. It's easy to say we are devoted to God, but true discipleship requires consistently living out our faith. This includes treating others kindly, showing integrity, and living according to biblical principles.

Just as we invest time and effort into nurturing human relationships, we must also nurture our relationship with God. This requires daily prayer, studying Scripture, and being open to the Holy Spirit's guidance. When we actively pursue a deeper connection with God, we grow stronger in our devotion.

True devotion doesn't waver under challenging times. Our faith and commitment to God are tested when we face trials or challenges. Remaining steadfast in our love for Him, even when circumstances are challenging, shows that we trust Him wholeheartedly.

Consistency In Faith

As disciples of Christ, we are called to remain consistent in our walk with God, especially in our faith. Our consistency builds spiritual endurance and resilience.

Consistency in faith involves a daily commitment to prayer, reading Scripture, and living out our beliefs. It's not just about following God when things are going well, but also seeking Him in times of uncertainty or trial. This steadfastness allows us to grow spiritually and remain anchored in our relationship with God.

Being consistent in faith means allowing it to influence every aspect of our lives—how we work, treat others, and respond to challenges.

Proper consistency in faith is demonstrated through our actions, showing that we are committed to living according to God's will. Difficult times will test our faith, but consistency helps us navigate these challenges. By holding firm to our trust in God's promises, we can face adversity with hope and courage.

Just as God is faithful, we are called to remain loyal to Him.

Consistent faith leads to spiritual growth. By regularly seeking God and applying His Word to our lives, we become more mature in our relationship with Him. Knowing that our foundation is Christ helps us handle life's challenges with wisdom and peace.

The Discipleship Journey

Discipleship is not a one-time event but a lifelong learning journey and a way of growing in faith. As disciples, we must continually seek a deeper understanding of God, His Word, and His will for our lives.

Scripture reveals God's character, promises, and guidance for our lives. Immersing ourselves in God's Word gives us wisdom, clarity, and insight into His will for our lives.

Prayer is another essential part of the discipleship journey. Through prayer, we communicate with God, seek His guidance, and align our hearts with His will.

Prayer deepens our relationship with God and helps us discern His direction. Disclpleship also involves growing within a community of believers.

Fellowship with other Christians allows us to encourage, support, and challenge one another in our walk with God. Being part of a faith community helps us stay accountable and motivated in our spiritual growth.

Growth often comes through challenges. As we face difficulties and obstacles, we learn to rely more on God and trust His plans. These experiences help us develop perseverance, strengthen our faith, and mature as believers.

Transformation Through The Holy Spirit

One of the most significant aspects of discipleship is the

transformative work of the Holy Spirit within us. When we commit to following Christ, the Holy Spirit renews and reshapes our hearts, minds, and lives.

Romans 12:2 reminds us, "Do not conform to the pattern of this world but be transformed by the renewing of your mind" (NIV). This means that as disciples, we are called to reject worldly values and embrace godly principles.

The Holy Spirit works within us to renew our thinking, aligning our thoughts and attitudes with God's truth. This renewal helps us discern God's will and empowers us to make decisions that reflect His character.

As the Holy Spirit transforms us, we begin to reflect the character of Christ in our daily lives.

The fruit of the Spirit— *"love, joy, peace, patience, kindness, goodness, faithfulness, gentleness, and self-control"* (Galatians 5:22-23, NIV)—becomes more evident as we grow in our relationship with God.

This transformation helps us live in a way that honors God and positively impacts those around us. The Holy Spirit also empowers us to overcome sin and weakness.

While imperfect, the Spirit enables us to resist temptation and obey God's Word. We are equipped to grow in holiness and righteousness through the Holy Spirit's power.

Transformation through the Holy Spirit is a lifelong process. As we continue to walk with Christ, the Spirit gradually shapes us into the image of Jesus. This ongoing transformation work helps us grow in faith, deepen our relationship with God, and live out our calling as disciples of Christ.

The Reward Of Discipleship

One of the most profound rewards of discipleship is the closeness we experience with God. We understand His love, faithfulness, and guidance as we draw nearer to Him.

"Draw near to God, and He will draw near to you." (James 4:8, NIV)

This closeness brings a deep sense of peace and security, reminding us that we are never alone. Knowing that God is present can bring tremendous comfort in times of distress.

"God is our refuge and strength, an ever-present help in trouble." (Psalm 46:1, NIV)

As disciples, we are assured that God walks with us through every trial, offering comfort, strength, and wisdom when needed. Experiencing God's presence also guides us as we navigate life's challenges.

When we seek God's presence through prayer and Scripture, He directs our paths and helps us make decisions by His will.

God's presence strengthens us for the daily challenges of life.

"Those who hope in the Lord will renew their strength." (Isaiah 40:31, NIV)

As disciples, we can tap into the power of God's presence, knowing His strength is perfect in our weakness (2 Corinthians 12:9). The more we experience God's presence, the deeper our relationship with Him becomes.

This intimacy grows as we pray, worship, and study His Word.

Over time, we know God's heart more fully and understand His desires for our lives. As our faith grows, we naturally become conduits of God's love to those around us.

Our actions, words, and choices reflect the light of Christ, allowing others to see His love through us.

Our commitment to discipleship sets an example for those searching for hope or truth.

People often watch how we handle challenges, show kindness, and remain steadfast in our faith. When we embody the principles of discipleship, we have the potential to draw others toward Christ.

Whether through sharing our testimony, offering a listening ear, or providing encouragement, our lives can serve as a bridge that leads others to experience God's love and grace for themselves.

The impact of our discipleship extends beyond our relationship with God. As we grow in our faith, we are called to make disciples of others (Matthew 28:19).

By mentoring, teaching, and encouraging fellow believers, we help build up the body of Christ, creating a ripple effect that touches the lives of many.

Counting The Cost

Jesus uses the analogy of building a tower to highlight the importance of counting costs before committing to discipleship.

Just as a builder must assess whether they have the resources to complete their project, we must consider what it means to follow Christ.

Discipleship requires sacrifices—giving up certain comforts, facing opposition, or placing God's will above our desires.

Discipleship is not a casual commitment; it involves completely transforming our lives.

"Seek first His kingdom and His righteousness." (Matthew 6:33, NIV)

Our faith should precede our daily activities, responsibilities, and desires. Everything else falls into place when we make God the center of our lives.

To truly prioritize our walk with Jesus, we may need to assess our current commitments. Are there activities or relationships that distract us from our spiritual growth?

Evaluating how we spend our time allows us to identify areas where we can make adjustments, ensuring we allocate sufficient time for prayer, studying Scripture, and fellowship with other believers.

Setting priorities often requires making hard choices. This might involve saying no to specific engagements, reducing time spent on social media, or limiting other distractions that pull us away from God.

By intentionally carving out time for Him, we cultivate a stronger relationship and grow spiritually. When we prioritize our relationship with God, we can trust that He will meet our needs.

We align ourselves with His will and purpose by seeking His kingdom first. This trust frees us from anxiety about the future, as we recognize that God is faithful in providing for us in all aspects of life.

The Joy Of Sacrifice

When we prioritize our relationship with Jesus, the things we give up—whether time, comfort, or specific desires—pale compared to the joy and fulfillment we find in Him. This perspective helps us view sacrifices not as burdens but as opportunities to deepen our connection with God.

Embracing the cost of discipleship transforms our understanding of sacrifice. Instead of seeing it as a loss, we view it as a chance for growth and greater intimacy with Christ.

Every act of sacrifice can draw us closer to Him, teaching us to depend on His strength and grace. As we sacrifice for our faith, we can cultivate a heart of gratitude.

Living With Purpose

Recognizing the blessings from our commitment to Christ allows us to rejoice in our journey. We learn to appreciate the small victories and the ways God provides for us in our obedience.

When we joyfully embrace the sacrifices of discipleship, we often witness God at work in our lives and the lives of others.

Our willingness to give up certain things can inspire those around us, encouraging them to explore their relationship with Christ.

Our joy in sacrifice can testify to God's goodness and faithfulness. Discipleship invites us to be part of God's mission to share His love and truth with others.

As we grow in our faith, we realize that our lives are not just about ourselves but about contributing to a larger story. This sense of purpose helps us understand that every action can significantly impact those around us, no matter how small.

When we live with purpose, we find fulfillment in serving others. Whether through acts of kindness, sharing the Gospel, or supporting our community, these acts become expressions of our faith.

"For we are God's handiwork, created in Christ Jesus to do good works, which God prepared in advance for us to do." (Ephesians 2:10, NIV)

Knowing that our lives have purpose motivates us to persevere through challenges.

Discipleship equips us with strength and resilience, enabling us to face difficulties with hope.

"I press on toward the goal to win the prize for which God has called me heavenward in Christ Jesus." (Philippians 3:14, NIV)

This promise fuels our determination to keep moving forward, even when the road is tough.

Our purpose in discipleship reminds us that our lives extend beyond the present. When we view our actions in light of eternity, we become more intentional about spending our time and resources. This perspective shifts our priorities and helps us focus on what truly matters—investing in relationships and spreading God's love.

Living purposefully naturally inspires others to do the same. Our passion for God's mission can ignite a fire in those around us, encouraging them to seek their purpose in Christ.

CHAPTER ELEVEN

YOUR IDENTITY
IN CHRIST

W e are made in the image of God. This means we have inherent worth and dignity.

Recognizing this truth helps us see ourselves through God's eyes, not through the lens of our mistakes or failures.

"Therefore, if anyone is in Christ, he is a new creation. The old has passed away; behold, the new has come." (2 Corinthians 5:17, NIV)

When we accept Christ, our past no longer defines us. We are given a fresh start, filled with hope and potential.

"But to all who did receive him, who believed in his name, he gave the right to become children of God." (John 1:12, NIV)

Accepting Christ means we are adopted into God's family. This identity comes with the privileges and responsibilities of being His children. As children of God, we are also heirs to His promises.

Our identity in Christ is secure because it is based on God's unchanging love.

"For I am convinced that neither death nor life, neither angels nor demons, neither the present nor the future, nor any powers, neither

height nor depth nor anything else in all creation, will be able to separate us from the love of God that is in Christ Jesus our Lord." (Romans 8:38-39, NIV)

No matter our circumstances, we can find comfort in knowing he deeply loves us. In Christ, we receive forgiveness for our sins.

Our identity is not defined by our failures but by God's grace. This truth frees us from guilt and shame, allowing us to live confidently in our new identity.

Understanding our identity in Christ calls us to live by faith.

"I have been crucified with Christ. It is no longer I who live, but Christ who lives in me." (Galatians 2:20, NIV)

We rely on Christ's strength to live out our identity daily. As followers of Christ, we are called to reflect His love to others.

Our lives should shine with Christ's love, bringing hope and encouragement to those around us. Knowing who we are in Christ gives us confidence. Knowing our identity is rooted in Him, we can face challenges with courage.

Our identity in Christ gives us purpose. We are designed to fulfill specific purposes that reflect God's glory in the world.

Knowing Your Worth As God's Arrow

God has given us specific gifts and talents that serve His purpose. These abilities are not random; they are part of His divine plan.

When we discover and develop our abilities, we fulfill our role in God's design. Each individual plays a crucial role in the larger tapestry of God's creation. Just as different parts of the body work together, our unique contributions are essential for the functioning of the body of Christ.

Recognizing our place in God's plan helps us appreciate the

importance of collaboration and unity within the community of believers.

Embracing God's design for our lives fosters self-acceptance. We often compare ourselves to others, but each person's journey and purpose are distinct.

"Each one should test their actions. Then they can take pride in themselves alone, without comparing themselves to someone else." (Galatians 6:4, NIV)

Accepting ourselves as God made us frees us to focus on our growth and contribution. Just as arrows are made for specific targets, we have a unique mission in life. Recognizing our mission empowers us to live out our purpose with confidence.

Our Worth In Christ

Our worth is rooted in our identity as children of God. This relationship is foundational, reminding us that we are cherished and valued by our Creator.

"For God so loved the world that he gave his one and only Son." (John 3:16, NIV)

This incredible sacrifice reveals our inherent worth, showing that we are valuable enough for God to give His Son for our redemption.

Our significance comes not from what we do but from who we are in Him. We can break free from the comparison trap when we recognize our worth in Christ.

Understanding that we are uniquely designed for a purpose helps us appreciate our journeys without measuring ourselves against others.

"No, in all these things we are more than conquerors through him who loved us." (Romans 8:37, NIV)

Embracing our inherent worth empowers us to live confidently. Knowing we are loved and valued by God enables us to pursue our purpose without fear of failure or rejection.

Glorifying God

Our primary purpose as followers of Christ is to glorify God in all we do.

"Whatever you do, whether in word or deed, do it all in the name of the Lord Jesus." (Colossians 3:17, NIV)

Every action, big or small, should reflect our faith and love for God. Our actions become vessels for His love and grace when we aim to glorify God.

By living out our faith authentically, we can point others to God and show His character through our lives. Bringing glory to God involves seeking His will in our decisions and actions.

"And we know that in all things God works for the good of those who love him." (Romans 8:28, NIV)

Even in difficult times, we can trust that our struggles can lead to growth and a deeper understanding of His goodness, ultimately bringing glory to Him.

Living for God's glory has eternal significance. Our purpose also includes reaching others with the message of Christ. Knowing our worth as arrows motivates us to share the hope and love of Jesus with those around us.

Overcoming Self-Doubt

Self-doubt often stems from feelings of inadequacy or comparison with others. However, we must remember that God has uniquely equipped us for the mission He has given us.

We can hold onto this promise when self-doubt creeps in, knowing that our journey is part of His divine plan. We must challenge and replace negative thoughts with God's truth to combat self-doubt.

When we focus on God's promises and remind ourselves of our worth in Him, we shift our mindset from doubt to faith.

"Trust in the Lord with all your heart and lean not on your understanding; in all your ways submit to him, and he will make your paths straight." (Proverbs 3:5-6, NIV)

Battling self-doubt often requires us to take steps of faith, even when we feel unsure. By acting on our faith and trusting in God's guidance, we can push through our doubts and experience growth and fulfillment in our mission.

Instead of comparing ourselves to others, we should focus on the strengths God has given us. Embracing our strengths helps us understand our unique role in God's plan.

Knowing our worth as God's arrow compels us to take action. We must live out our purpose by engaging in good works and sharing God's love. As we step out in faith, we must trust God to direct our paths.

Targeting Giants With Purpose

The first step in confronting giants is to recognize them in our lives. These giants can manifest in various ways, such as fear, doubt, addiction, financial struggles, or damaging relationships.

Just as David faced Goliath, we must identify our battles to prepare for the fight. Acknowledging our giants can be uncomfortable, but it's essential for growth. We can confront these challenges rather than allow them to linger in the shadows by bringing them into the open. This process often involves honest reflection and prayer, seeking God's guidance to uncover our overwhelmed areas. Recognizing the influence of these giants is crucial.

How do they affect our lives, decisions, and relationships?

For example, fear might keep us from pursuing opportunities, while addiction could lead to isolation. Understanding their impact allows us to see the need for change and motivates us to take action.

Once we identify our giants, we must seek God's perspective.

"We seemed like grasshoppers in our own eyes and looked the same to them." (Numbers 13:33, NIV)

We often view ourselves as insignificant compared to our giants, but we must remember that God is more significant than any challenge we face. When we recognize that our giants are not impossible, we can begin to take proactive steps to address them.

This may involve setting boundaries in negative relationships, seeking addiction support, or developing a plan to overcome financial struggles.

Just as David prepared to fight Goliath with a sling and stones, we, too, need to equip ourselves with the tools and strategies to confront our giants. Reflecting on past victories helps build our faith and confidence in God's ability to help us conquer current challenges.

"David said, 'The Lord who rescued me from the paw of the lion and the paw of the bear will rescue me from the hand of this Philistine.'" (1 Samuel 17:34-37, NIV)

In Ephesians 6:10-18, Apostle Paul describes the spiritual armor God provides to protect us in our battles. This includes the belt of truth, the breastplate of righteousness, the shoes of readiness, the shield of faith, the helmet of salvation, and the sword of the Spirit.

Each piece serves a vital purpose, helping us stand firm against our challenges. In our journey to confront giants, seeking God's guidance is crucial. This involves asking Him for clarity, wisdom, and strength as we navigate our challenges.

Equipping ourselves spiritually involves not just preparation but also action. Just as David actively faced Goliath with his sling and stones, we must take steps to confront our giants. This may mean addressing unhealthy habits, stepping out of our comfort zones, or actively working to overcome our fears.

David didn't shy away from Goliath but stepped forward in faith. Similarly, we must confront our giants with courage.

Speaking Life Into Your Situation

Just as David confidently declared his faith in God's power before facing Goliath, we can, too, bring life to our situations by proclaiming God's promises.

"Come," David said, "and I'll give your flesh to the birds of the sky and the beasts of the field!" But David said to the Philistine, "You come against me with sword and spear and javelin, but I come against you in the name of the Lord Almighty, the God of the armies of Israel, whom you have defied." (1 Samuel 17:45-47, NIV)

Scripture is filled with assurances of God's faithfulness, love, and strength.

By declaring these truths over our lives, we invite God's presence into our circumstances and shift our focus from fear to faith.

Understanding who you are in Christ is essential for speaking life into your situation.

"For we are God's handiwork, created in Christ Jesus to do good works, which God prepared in advance for us to do." (Ephesians 2:10, NIV)

Recognizing your worth and identity as a child of God empowers you to speak positively about your circumstances, knowing that

God has a purpose for your life.

What we say reflects our thoughts. To speak life, we must fill our minds with the truth of God's Word.

Meditating on Scripture helps replace negative thoughts with affirmations of God's goodness and faithfulness. When facing challenges, giving in to fear and doubt is easy. However, we must choose to speak words of faith instead.

"For the Spirit God gave us does not make us timid, but gives us power, love, and self-discipline." (2 Timothy 1:7, NIV)

Uplifting Others with Life-Giving Words

Speaking life isn't just about our situations; it also involves uplifting those around us.

"Gracious words are a honeycomb, sweet to the soul and healing to the bones." (Proverbs 16:24, NIV)

When we encourage others with positive words and affirmations of faith, we create an environment where everyone can thrive and grow in their relationship with God.

Speaking life goes hand-in-hand with taking action. Just as David prepared for battle and acted on his faith, we must be willing to take steps toward our goals and trust God to work through our efforts.

"As the body without the spirit is dead, so faith without deeds is dead." (James 2:26, NIV)

When we proclaim God's promises and actively pursue our goals, we trust His ability to deliver.

Celebrating Victory and Inspiring Others

The journey to overcoming giants often involves struggles and setbacks. We should view our battles as opportunities for growth and learning, helping us to develop a deeper faith.

After defeating Goliath, David didn't just move on; he celebrated his victory. We need to recognize and celebrate our wins, no matter how small. Acknowledging our progress boosts our morale and motivates us to continue targeting our giants.

Just as David's victory inspired the Israelites, our victories can inspire those around us.

"The Israelites pursued the Philistines, striking them down and killing them along the way." (1 Samuel 17:51-52, NIV)

Sharing our testimonies of overcoming giants encourages others to confront their challenges with faith.

CONCLUSION

The Call To Leave A Mark

We are unique, created with specific gifts and talents that can contribute to the greater good.

"For we are God's handiwork, created in Christ Jesus to do good works, which God prepared in advance for us to do." (Ephesians 2:10, NIV)

Embracing this truth helps us understand that we have a purpose beyond ourselves. We must seek God's plan for our lives to leave a mark. This involves prayer, reflection, and a willingness to listen.

When we align our actions with God's will, we can be instruments of His love and grace, impacting those around us. Every small act of kindness can create a ripple effect.

"Whatever you do, do your work heartily, as for the Lord, not for human masters, knowing that from the Lord you will receive the inheritance as your reward. You serve the Lord Christ." (Colossians 3:23-24, NIV)

Leaving a mark often means choosing to love others unconditionally.

"Love is patient, love is kind. It does not envy, it does not boast, it is not

proud. It does not dishonor others, it is not self-seeking, it is not easily angered, it keeps no record of wrongs." (1 Corinthians 13:4-5, NIV)

Embodying these traits creates a positive environment that encourages others to grow and thrive. Our personal stories of faith and growth can inspire others.

"They triumphed over him by the blood of the Lamb and by the word of their testimony." (Revelation 12:11, NIV)

Creating a Positive Environment

To leave a mark, we should create environments where others feel safe to share their stories. This means listening without judgment, offering support, and being present.

When people feel valued and understood, they are more likely to open up and share their journeys. A radical life often involves advocating for justice and standing against injustice.

"He has shown you, O mortal, what is good. And what does the Lord require of you? To act justly and to love mercy and to walk humbly with your God." (Micah 6:8, NIV)

We can leave a mark that reflects God's heart by being voices for the voiceless and advocating for those in need. Leaving a mark also means empowering others to realize their potential.

"In everything I did, I showed you that by this kind of hard work, we must help the weak, remembering the words the Lord Jesus himself said: 'It is more blessed to give than to receive.'" (Acts 20:35, NIV)

To leave a lasting mark, we must consistently live out our values.

"Do not merely listen to the word, and so deceive yourselves. Do what it says." (James 1:22, NIV)

Modeling Faith and Values

Our actions speak louder than words. Living out our faith authentically makes us role models for younger generations.

"Start children off on the way they should go, and even when they are old, they will not turn from it." (Proverbs 22:6, NIV)

We guide them in their spiritual journeys by embodying the principles of faith, love, and integrity. In a world often driven by material success, it's essential to emphasize values that truly matter.

"Do not store up for yourselves treasures on earth, where moths and vermin destroy, and where thieves break in and steal. But store up for yourselves treasures in heaven." (Matthew 6:19-20, NIV)

Investing in Relationships

Relationships are the foundation of a healthy community. By nurturing strong connections with family, friends, and mentors, we create a support system for future generations.

"Two are better than one, because they have a good return for their labor: If either of them falls, one can help the other up." (Ecclesiastes 4:9-10, NIV)

Investing in relationships shows younger generations the importance of love, support, and collaboration. Encouraging open conversations is vital for growth.

"As iron sharpens iron, so one person sharpens another." (Proverbs 27:17, NIV)

Empowering Future Generations

Standing tall for future generations means empowering them to take the lead.

"Don't let anyone look down on you because you are young, but set an example for the believers in speech, in conduct, in love, in faith, and purity." (1 Timothy 4:12, NIV)

We foster their growth and confidence by allowing them to serve, lead, and express their creativity.

Education and wisdom are powerful tools. By teaching young

people about God's Word, we equip them with the knowledge they need to navigate life's challenges.

"Teach them to your children, talking about them when you sit at home and when you walk along the road, when you lie down and when you get up." (Deuteronomy 6:7, NIV)

Standing tall also involves advocating for justice and compassion in our communities. Addressing poverty, inequality, and injustice teaches future generations the importance of standing up for what is right.

"He has shown you, O mortal, what is good. And what does the Lord require of you? To act justly and to love mercy and to walk humbly with your God." (Micah 6:8, NIV)

When we actively participate in community service and advocacy, we show young people the importance of giving back. This commitment to serving others instills a sense of responsibility and encourages them to continue this legacy of compassion and action.

Life will have its challenges, and it's crucial to teach future generations the importance of perseverance.

"Whatever you do, do your work heartily, as for the Lord rather than for men." (Colossians 3:23, NASB)

By demonstrating a solid work ethic and resilience in adversity, we prepare young people to tackle life's obstacles confidently. It's essential to frame failures as opportunities for growth. By sharing our experiences of overcoming challenges, we help young people understand that setbacks are part of life.

"We also glory in our sufferings, because we know that suffering produces perseverance; perseverance, character; and character, hope." (Romans 5:3-4, NIV)

Sharing our stories, experiences, and faith journeys can create a treasure trove of wisdom for future generations.

Passing down our testimonies, whether through written records, videos, or family gatherings, ensures that they have a source of inspiration and guidance.

"One generation commends your works to another, and they proclaim your mighty acts." (Psalm 145:4, NIV)

Encouraging a culture of gratitude ensures that future generations appreciate the blessings in their lives. Teaching them to recognize God's goodness in big and small moments cultivates a spirit of thankfulness that will guide them throughout their lives.

"Give thanks in all circumstances; for this is God's will for you in Christ Jesus." (1 Thessalonians 5:18, NIV)

A SPECIAL CALL TO SALVATION & NEW BEGINNINGS FROM APOSTLE DR. DAVID PHILEMON

Dear Beloved,

God loves you deeply and has brought you to this moment for a reason. No matter your past, His love and forgiveness are available to you.

The Bible says in John 3:16, "For God so loved the world that He gave His one and only Son, that whoever believes in Him shall not perish but have eternal life." Jesus Christ came to save you, offering you a new life of purpose and peace.

If you're ready to accept Jesus as your Lord and Savior, pray this simple prayer:

The Salvation Prayer

"Heavenly Father, I come to You in the Name of Jesus. I acknowledge that I am a sinner in need of a Savior. I believe that Jesus Christ is Your Son, that He died for my sins, and that You raised Him from the dead. I repent of my sins and turn to You with my

Whole heart. Jesus, I ask You to come into my life. Be my Lord and my Savior. I surrender my life to You. Fill me with Your Holy Spirit, guide me on the path of righteousness, and help me to follow Your script for my life. Thank you, Father, for saving me. In the name of Jesus. Amen."

Welcome to the Family of God!

If you have just prayed this prayer, Congratulations! You are now a child of God, and heaven is rejoicing. Your journey has begun, and we're here to support you as you grow in faith and discover God's unique plans for you.

Next Steps:

• Connect with a Bible-believing church.
• Read the Bible Daily: God's Word is your guide.
• Pray Regularly: Prayer is your lifeline to God.
• Share Your Faith: Don't keep the good news to yourself.

www.ingramcontent.com/pod-product-compliance
Lightning Source LLC
Chambersburg PA
CBHW071859020426
42331CB00010B/2588